Magic & Love. Ma

Practical magic, love spells, enchantments, and mystical practices for attaining love

Annabel Arno

Copyright © 2024 by Annabel Arno

All rights reserved.

No portion of this book may be reproduced in any form without written permission from the publisher or author, except as permitted by U.S. copyright law.

This publication is designed to provide accurate and authoritative information in regard to the subject matter covered. It is sold with the understanding that neither the author nor the publisher is engaged in rendering legal, investment, accounting or other professional services. While the publisher and author have used their best efforts in preparing this book, they make no representations or warranties with respect to the accuracy or completeness of the contents of this book and specifically disclaim any implied warranties of merchantability or fitness for a particular purpose. No warranty may be created or extended by sales representatives or written sales materials. The advice and strategies contained herein may not be suitable for your situation. You should consult with a professional when appropriate. Neither the publisher nor the author shall be liable for any loss of profit or any other commercial damages, including but not limited to special, incidental, consequential, personal, or other damages.

- Introduction 4
- Part I: Foundations of Magical Love 6
- Chapter 1: The Alchemy of Love 6
  - Introduction to the Magical Dimension of Love 6
  - Understanding Love from a Mystical Perspective 8
  - Exploring the Connection Between Magic and Love 10
  - The Energetic Dynamics of Romantic Relationships 12
  - A Brief Overview of the Historical and Cultural Context of Love Magic 14
  - The Philosophy Behind Magical Practices in Love 16
- Chapter 2: Preparing the Self for Magical Love 18
  - Self-Love as the Foundation for Relationship Magic 18
  - Cleansing and Purification Rituals for the Heart and Spirit 19
  - Aligning with the Intention of True Love 24
  - Exercises and Rituals to Cultivate Self-Love 26
- Chapter 3: The Basics of Magical Practice 29
  - A Beginner's Guide to Magic and Its Principles 29
  - How to Set Intentions and Choose the Right Magical Methods for Love 31
  - Tools and Symbols Commonly Used in Love Magic and Creating Sacred Space for Magical Work 33
- Part II: Attracting Love 36
- Chapter 4: Preparing for New Love 36
  - Clearing Past Energies and Emotional Baggage 36
  - Rituals for Opening the Heart to New Love 44
- Chapter 5: The Art of Love Spells 47
  - An Introduction to Love Spells and Their Purpose 47
  - Step-by-Step Guides for Simple Love Spells 48
  - Detailed Guide on Love-Attracting Spells 51
  - Customizing Spells for Individual Needs 53
- Chapter 6: Enchantments and Charms 55
  - How to Create and Charge Talismans and Amulets for Love 55
  - The Use of Herbs, Oils, and Candles in Love Enchantments 57
  - Maintaining and Storing Magical Objects 60
- Chapter 7: Mystical Practices for Love 62
  - Meditation and Visualization Techniques for Attracting Love 62
  - Astrology in Love 64
  - Using Dream Work to Reveal Insights About Relationships 65

Part III: The Magic of Connection 68
Chapter 8: Strengthening Bonds 68
- Magical Practices for Deepening Intimacy and Trust 68
- Communication Spells and Rituals to Enhance Understanding 69
- A Magical Approach to Attracting a Man's Attention in Communication 73

Chapter 9: Keeping the Flame Alive 76
- Magic for Rekindling Passion and Interest 76
- Celebratory Rituals for Anniversaries and Special Occasions 78

Part IV: Overcoming Love's Challenges 81
Chapter 10: Navigating Relationship Challenges 81
- When to Use Magic and When to Seek Mundane Solutions 81
- Protection Spells for Safeguarding Love 83
- Letting Go and Moving On: Dealing with Unrequited Love Through Magic 85

Part V: Ethical Considerations and Advanced Practices 88
Chapter 11: The Ethics of Love Magic 88
- Discussion on the Moral Implications of Love Spells 88
- Respecting Free Will and Consent in Magical Practices 90
- Understanding the Moral Implications of Influencing Will 91
- The Karmic Considerations of Love Spells 93

Chapter 12: Advanced Magical Work 95
- Working with Deities and Spirits in Love Magic 95
- Creating Long-Term Talismans for Love and Relationship Stability 97

Afterword and Conclusion 100
Appendices 102
- A Glossary of Magical Terms 102
- Step-by-Step Guides for Rituals and Spells 104

Introduction

Welcome, dear reader, to a realm where the whispers of the heart echo with the ancient chants of magic. "Magic & Love. Magical Match" invites you on an odyssey that explores the interplay of mystical forces within the sacred dance of relationships. This book is more than a collection of words; it is a vessel of transformation for the soul seeking the sweet nectar of love in its purest form.

Love is the invisible force that binds the tapestry of our lives. It is the wellspring of joy, the balm for pain, and the most profound connection to the spiritual dimensions of our existence. Our relationships—romantic, platonic, and all the intricate variations therein—shape our journey, color our experiences, and contribute to our growth. In every heart lies the desire for a connection that resonates with the rhythms of the universe, a desire to love and be loved unconditionally and profoundly.

Yet, love's landscape can be as complex as it is enchanting. This is where the age-old wisdom of magical methods comes to light. Within this book, you'll discover the symbiosis of love and magic, a harmonious blend of practices that date back to the mystics and sages of old. We delve into the tapestry of love magic—a tapestry rich with spells, rituals, and incantations designed to attract, nurture, and heal relationships.

"Magic & Love. Magical Match" provides an illuminating overview of these mystical traditions, revealing how they can be woven into the modern fabric of love and partnership. As we journey through the chapters, you'll learn how to harness the elements, draw on the power of symbols, and invoke the energies that align with your intentions for love. Whether it's the simple magic of a candlelit dinner or the profound ritual of a love-binding spell, the magic here is accessible to all, adept and novice alike.

Embark on this transformative journey with an open heart. Here, we blend the eternal quest for love with the potent mysteries of the unseen, creating a path to a love that is as enchanted as it is real. Prepare to discover the alchemy of the heart, the secret convergence where all our personal stories of love are written in the stars and where your "Magical Match" awaits—a union of passion, depth, and destiny, conjured by the very essence of magic and love.

Part I: Foundations of Magical Love

Chapter 1: The Alchemy of Love

Introduction to the Magical Dimension of Love

In every culture, across every era, love has been revered as the most potent and profound force—a universal language that speaks to the deepest part of our human essence. Yet, there is an element to love that transcends the mere physical and emotional. It enters the realm of the mystical, where the energies we emit and the connections we forge are more than just coincidences; they are part of a magical tapestry that the universe orchestrates. This is the magical dimension of love, a space where the heart's desires are whispered to the stars and manifested into reality through the ancient art of practical magic, love spells, enchantments, and mystical practices.

Consider for a moment the electrifying moment when two gazes meet and there is an undeniable spark, a sense of knowing, a pull that defies explanation. This is not just chemistry—it is the dance of energies, an interaction of auras, a silent conversation between souls. In the magical dimension, love is energy. It is the same force that moves the tides and guides the phases of the moon. Understanding this energy is the first step in unlocking the magic of love.

Practical magic is the use of this energy and these universal forces in a focused, intentional way to bring about change. It's the whispered intention behind a gift to a loved one, the carefully selected date of a wedding aligned with the lunar cycle, or

Part I: Foundations of Magical Love

Chapter 1: The Alchemy of Love

Introduction to the Magical Dimension of Love

In every culture, across every era, love has been revered as the most potent and profound force—a universal language that speaks to the deepest part of our human essence. Yet, there is an element to love that transcends the mere physical and emotional. It enters the realm of the mystical, where the energies we emit and the connections we forge are more than just coincidences; they are part of a magical tapestry that the universe orchestrates. This is the magical dimension of love, a space where the heart's desires are whispered to the stars and manifested into reality through the ancient art of practical magic, love spells, enchantments, and mystical practices.

Consider for a moment the electrifying moment when two gazes meet and there is an undeniable spark, a sense of knowing, a pull that defies explanation. This is not just chemistry—it is the dance of energies, an interaction of auras, a silent conversation between souls. In the magical dimension, love is energy. It is the same force that moves the tides and guides the phases of the moon. Understanding this energy is the first step in unlocking the magic of love.

Practical magic is the use of this energy and these universal forces in a focused, intentional way to bring about change. It's the whispered intention behind a gift to a loved one, the carefully selected date of a wedding aligned with the lunar cycle, or even the daily affirmation of one's worthiness of love and happiness. These acts are the threads of magic that are sewn into the fabric of everyday life.

Love spells, often misunderstood, are not about bending the will of another or forcing love to emerge. True love spells work by aligning one's personal energy with the energy of love, thus attracting it in its most authentic form. Consider a love spell as a letter sent out into the universe, declaring your readiness to love and be loved. It is an invitation, not a demand. The ingredients and rituals—be it a candle, a piece of paper, or a chant—are simply tools to focus your intention, to set your heartfelt desires into motion.

Enchantments for love might sound like the stuff of fairy tales, but they are deeply rooted in the natural world. It's in the way a rose quartz crystal is charged under the light of the full moon, ready to draw love closer. It's found in the daily ritual of wearing a perfume infused with intention, or in the anointing of a candle with oils that hold the essence of attraction.

In today's world, where the mystical often intertwines with the practical, ancient practices are being revived and reimagined. A tarot reading can provide insight into the path to love, and a meditation session focused on the heart chakra can clear blockages that are holding one back from fully embracing love.

Imagine Sarah, a young woman whose belief in the magic of love led her to light a pink candle every Friday night, with the simple intention of attracting the right person into her life. Or Michael, who, after a series of failed relationships, began a daily practice of affirming his worthiness of a healthy, fulfilling love. These are modern-day practitioners of love's magic, individuals who have tapped into the power that resides within them and within the universe.

The mystical perspective posits that everything is interconnected through universal energy. Love is the most potent connector in this energy web, drawing individuals together in a dynamic interplay of souls. Think of love as a dance where each person is both leading and following, giving and receiving, in a harmonious exchange of energies. This is the dance that aligns us with the rhythms of the universe, creating synchronicities and 'coincidences' that are often the universe's way of communicating with us.

Consider Anna, who practiced love meditation every morning, focusing on sending love to those in her life and to the world at large. Over time, she noticed that her relationships began to deepen and become more meaningful. Or take the case of John, who used visualization techniques to imagine the love he desired. Not long after, he met someone who matched the feelings and qualities he had visualized.

In many traditions, rituals are used to celebrate and honor the mystical aspect of love. Whether it's through handfasting ceremonies, which symbolically intertwine the lives of lovers, or the Japanese practice of Kintsugi, where broken pottery is mended with gold to celebrate the beauty of imperfection in love, these rituals remind us that love is a sacred contract that transcends the physical.

From a mystical standpoint, love has the power to transform. It is the alchemist's fire that turns leaden hearts into golden souls. It is the force that propels us to grow, to evolve, and to become more than we were. The transformative power of love can be seen in the way it inspires us to acts of kindness, to artistic creation, and to the betterment of ourselves and the world around us.

Understanding love from a mystical perspective allows us to see it not just as an emotion or a connection between two people, but as a magical and transformative energy that is part of a larger, universal tapestry. By aligning ourselves with the frequency of love, by honoring its sacred and ethereal qualities, and by engaging in rituals that celebrate its mystical nature, we open ourselves to a more profound, magical experience of love.

Exploring the Connection Between Magic and Love

The tapestry of human experience is interwoven with threads of love and strands of magic. These two ancient forces have danced together through time, each one drawing strength and purpose from the other. To explore the connection between magic and love is to delve into a rich history of human endeavor to understand, enhance, and celebrate the most profound of our emotions.

Love is inherently magical. It has the power to transform the ordinary into the extraordinary, to elevate our experiences and color our perceptions with deeper hues of meaning. Magic, in its essence, is the practice of influencing the fabric of reality through will and intention. When combined, the magic of intention and the power of love have the potential to create profound change in our lives.

Take, for example, the story of Emma, a young woman who believed deeply in the magic of love. She crafted a ritual to find her soulmate, focusing her intention on attracting a partner who was kind, loyal, and true. Within months of her ritual, she met Leo at a community event, and they felt an immediate connection. It was as if the universe had conspired to bring them together, guided by the magic of Emma's intent.

In every culture, there are rituals surrounding love and union. From the exchange of rings in wedding ceremonies to the less formal but equally significant rituals of a couple's first kiss or the regular date night, these are all forms of magic at work. They

- Part III: The Magic of Connection 68
- Chapter 8: Strengthening Bonds 68
  - Magical Practices for Deepening Intimacy and Trust 68
  - Communication Spells and Rituals to Enhance Understanding 69
  - A Magical Approach to Attracting a Man's Attention in Communication ... 73
- Chapter 9: Keeping the Flame Alive 76
  - Magic for Rekindling Passion and Interest 76
  - Celebratory Rituals for Anniversaries and Special Occasions 78
- Part IV: Overcoming Love's Challenges 81
- Chapter 10: Navigating Relationship Challenges 81
  - When to Use Magic and When to Seek Mundane Solutions 81
  - Protection Spells for Safeguarding Love 83
  - Letting Go and Moving On: Dealing with Unrequited Love Through Magic 85
- Part V: Ethical Considerations and Advanced Practices 88
- Chapter 11: The Ethics of Love Magic 88
  - Discussion on the Moral Implications of Love Spells 88
  - Respecting Free Will and Consent in Magical Practices 90
  - Understanding the Moral Implications of Influencing Will 91
  - The Karmic Considerations of Love Spells 93
- Chapter 12: Advanced Magical Work 95
  - Working with Deities and Spirits in Love Magic 95
  - Creating Long-Term Talismans for Love and Relationship Stability 97
- Afterword and Conclusion 100
- Appendices 102
- A Glossary of Magical Terms 102
- Step-by-Step Guides for Rituals and Spells 104

Introduction

Welcome, dear reader, to a realm where the whispers of the heart echo with the ancient chants of magic. "Magic & Love. Magical Match" invites you on an odyssey that explores the interplay of mystical forces within the sacred dance of relationships. This book is more than a collection of words; it is a vessel of transformation for the soul seeking the sweet nectar of love in its purest form.

Love is the invisible force that binds the tapestry of our lives. It is the wellspring of joy, the balm for pain, and the most profound connection to the spiritual dimensions of our existence. Our relationships—romantic, platonic, and all the intricate variations therein—shape our journey, color our experiences, and contribute to our growth. In every heart lies the desire for a connection that resonates with the rhythms of the universe, a desire to love and be loved unconditionally and profoundly.

Yet, love's landscape can be as complex as it is enchanting. This is where the age-old wisdom of magical methods comes to light. Within this book, you'll discover the symbiosis of love and magic, a harmonious blend of practices that date back to the mystics and sages of old. We delve into the tapestry of love magic—a tapestry rich with spells, rituals, and incantations designed to attract, nurture, and heal relationships.

"Magic & Love. Magical Match" provides an illuminating overview of these mystical traditions, revealing how they can be woven into the modern fabric of love and partnership. As we journey through the chapters, you'll learn how to harness the elements, draw on the power of symbols, and invoke the energies that align with your intentions for love. Whether it's the simple magic of a candlelit dinner or the profound ritual of a love-binding spell, the magic here is accessible to all, adept and novice alike.

Embark on this transformative journey with an open heart. Here, we blend the eternal quest for love with the potent mysteries of the unseen, creating a path to a love that is as enchanted as it is real. Prepare to discover the alchemy of the heart, the secret convergence where all our personal stories of love are written in the stars and where your "Magical Match" awaits—a union of passion, depth, and destiny, conjured by the very essence of magic and love.

As we embark on this journey together, remember that the magic of love is not found in grand gestures or elaborate spells—it's in the intention, the belief, and the openness to let love unfold in its own divine time. The magic of love and relationships is as accessible as it is mysterious, and with each page turned, we will delve deeper into understanding how to tap into this timeless wisdom.

Understanding Love from a Mystical Perspective

The journey of love is as mystical as it is grounded in reality. To understand love from a mystical perspective is to recognize it as a force that not only creates bonds between people but also connects us to the greater cosmos. It is a profound energy that transcends the physical world and taps into the spiritual and the esoteric.

Love, in its essence, is ethereal. It is not confined to the tangible elements of the world but exists in the liminal spaces where feelings and energies reside. Mystics and sages throughout history have spoken of love as the ultimate truth, the fundamental energy that is both the source and the destination of all life's journeys. From the Sufi poets who saw divine love as the ultimate connection to the cosmos, to the Celtic druids who believed that love was the force that intertwined the fates of all beings, love's mystical nature has been revered.

On a metaphysical level, love emits the highest vibrational frequency. Emotions like fear, anger, and jealousy exist at lower frequencies, while love, joy, and gratitude vibrate higher. Engaging in love's high vibration means elevating oneself above the mundane, above the negative energies that can often entangle us. This is why when we are in love, we feel uplifted, as if we are in harmony with the pulse of the universe.

The mystical perspective posits that everything is interconnected through universal energy. Love is the most potent connector in this energy web, drawing individuals together in a dynamic interplay of souls. Think of love as a dance where each person is both leading and following, giving and receiving, in a harmonious exchange of energies. This is the dance that aligns us with the rhythms of the universe, creating synchronicities and 'coincidences' that are often the universe's way of communicating with us.

Consider Anna, who practiced love meditation every morning, focusing on sending love to those in her life and to the world at large. Over time, she noticed that her relationships began to deepen and become more meaningful. Or take the case of John, who used visualization techniques to imagine the love he desired. Not long after, he met someone who matched the feelings and qualities he had visualized.

In many traditions, rituals are used to celebrate and honor the mystical aspect of love. Whether it's through handfasting ceremonies, which symbolically intertwine the lives of lovers, or the Japanese practice of Kintsugi, where broken pottery is mended with gold to celebrate the beauty of imperfection in love, these rituals remind us that love is a sacred contract that transcends the physical.

From a mystical standpoint, love has the power to transform. It is the alchemist's fire that turns leaden hearts into golden souls. It is the force that propels us to grow, to evolve, and to become more than we were. The transformative power of love can be seen in the way it inspires us to acts of kindness, to artistic creation, and to the betterment of ourselves and the world around us.

Understanding love from a mystical perspective allows us to see it not just as an emotion or a connection between two people, but as a magical and transformative energy that is part of a larger, universal tapestry. By aligning ourselves with the frequency of love, by honoring its sacred and ethereal qualities, and by engaging in rituals that celebrate its mystical nature, we open ourselves to a more profound, magical experience of love.

Exploring the Connection Between Magic and Love

The tapestry of human experience is interwoven with threads of love and strands of magic. These two ancient forces have danced together through time, each one drawing strength and purpose from the other. To explore the connection between magic and love is to delve into a rich history of human endeavor to understand, enhance, and celebrate the most profound of our emotions.

Love is inherently magical. It has the power to transform the ordinary into the extraordinary, to elevate our experiences and color our perceptions with deeper hues of meaning. Magic, in its essence, is the practice of influencing the fabric of reality through will and intention. When combined, the magic of intention and the power of love have the potential to create profound change in our lives.

Take, for example, the story of Emma, a young woman who believed deeply in the magic of love. She crafted a ritual to find her soulmate, focusing her intention on attracting a partner who was kind, loyal, and true. Within months of her ritual, she met Leo at a community event, and they felt an immediate connection. It was as if the universe had conspired to bring them together, guided by the magic of Emma's intent.

In every culture, there are rituals surrounding love and union. From the exchange of rings in wedding ceremonies to the less formal but equally significant rituals of a couple's first kiss or the regular date night, these are all forms of magic at work. They are actions imbued with meaning and intent, designed to forge and reinforce bonds, to manifest and maintain the connection between two souls.

Historically, love spells have been cast by those wishing to summon love into their lives or to ensure its continuation and growth. While the ethics of love spells are much debated, the intent behind them is clear—to call forth the powerful energies of attraction and commitment. Love spells range from simple affirmations and visualization exercises to complex ceremonies involving multiple elements and phases of the moon.

The connection between magic and love can also be seen in the correspondences found in nature. Certain herbs, stones, and symbols are associated with love and are used to amplify love's presence and power. Rose quartz is often called the 'love stone' for its properties of promoting love and emotional healing. Similarly, roses are commonly associated with love, and their presence in a love spell or ritual is believed to draw in loving energy.

Across the globe, there are countless tales of love's magic at play. Consider the couple who writes down their hopes for their relationship during the new moon, and finds that by the full moon, their connection has deepened. Or the individual who carries a piece of rose quartz in their pocket as a reminder to open their heart, and then encounters a new love where they least expect it.

The connection between magic and love is a reminder that our deepest desires and our highest intentions can align to bring about the love we seek. Whether through traditional rituals or personal, meaningful practices, the magic we weave into our lives when it comes to love is both a reflection of our deepest selves and a bridge to the future we yearn for.

As we continue to explore the practical applications of love's magic, let us do so with a respect for the mystery, a commitment to the ethical, and an open heart ready to receive the love that is our birthright.

The Energetic Dynamics of Romantic Relationships

At the heart of every romantic encounter and enduring partnership lies an intricate dance of energy. The realm of romance is not just built upon mutual interests, physical attraction, or shared goals—it thrives on the dynamic interplay of energies that each person brings into the relationship. This chapter delves into the subtle, yet powerful, energetic dynamics that can often determine the success and depth of our romantic connections. Understanding these dynamics offers a form of practical magic that can be harnessed to foster love, heal wounds, and create a harmonious match.

Every individual radiates a unique vibrational frequency that reflects their emotional state, thoughts, and soul's essence. When two people meet, their energies begin a delicate tango, each one affecting and being affected by the other. A harmonious relationship is often a result of resonant frequencies that create a sense of ease, comfort, and compatibility. Conversely, dissonant frequencies can lead to conflicts, misunderstandings, and a general sense of unease.

Consider the story of Mia and Alex, who felt an immediate sense of familiarity and ease when they first met. Their energetic resonance allowed them to develop a deep connection with minimal effort. On the other hand, Laura and Jeff struggled with constant bickering despite their strong attraction to each other, a sign of their clashing energies that needed to be addressed and harmonized.

In the study of energetic anatomy, chakras are vital energy centers within the body that govern various aspects of our being. In the context of romantic relationships, the heart chakra plays a pivotal role, governing our capacity to give and receive love. A balanced heart chakra enables us to experience love in its purest form, fostering compassion, empathy, and a strong emotional bond with our partner.

Our emotional interactions create invisible energy cords that connect us to our partners. These cords can carry both positive feelings of love and support, as well as negative energies of past hurts and resentments. Practitioners of energy work believe in the importance of cleansing these cords to maintain a healthy relationship, employing methods such as meditation, visualization, and cord-cutting rituals when necessary.

Engaging in regular energy management practices can significantly improve the quality of a romantic relationship. Simple activities like spending time in nature together, practicing joint meditation, or even synchronizing breathing can align a couple's energies. For example, Rachel and Sam found that their weekly practice of couples yoga brought a newfound sense of harmony and understanding to their relationship.

It's crucial for individuals in a relationship to maintain their energetic boundaries and practice self-care. Overdependence on a partner for energetic stability can lead to imbalances and a loss of self-identity. Encouraging each other to engage in personal hobbies, spend time with friends, and pursue individual goals can help maintain a healthy energetic ecosystem within the relationship.

The energetic dynamics of romantic relationships are a complex yet beautiful aspect of love that can be influenced by practical magic and intentional practice. By understanding and nurturing these dynamics, couples can achieve a magical match

—a relationship where energies are aligned, challenges are navigated with wisdom, and love is deepened by the unseen yet palpable dance of the soul.

A Brief Overview of the Historical and Cultural Context of Love Magic

The quest for love is as old as humanity itself, and so is the use of magic to find, nurture, and protect it. Across the sands of time and the breadth of the world, nearly every civilization has had its own traditions of love magic. These practices, while diverse in their rituals and beliefs, all speak to a universal longing for connection and companionship.

The earliest records of love magic take us back to the ancients—Egyptians, Greeks, Romans, and beyond. The Egyptians, with their intricate spells and amulets, believed in the power of magic to secure both the favor of the gods and the heart of a beloved. The Greeks consulted oracles and used philtres—potions believed to enchant the drinker with love. The Romans, for their part, incorporated magic into their betrothals and weddings, invoking gods and goddesses of love to bless their unions.

Moving into the medieval era, the notion of courtly love flourished, and with it, a myriad of magical practices aimed at expressing and securing romantic affection. Troubadours sang not just of earthly love, but of a love that was divine and mystical in nature. Spells and charms of this period often included the use of herbs like rosemary and thyme, both thought to evoke the essence of love.

As we traverse the globe, we encounter a rich diversity of love magic. In West Africa, the Yoruba tradition speaks of Oshun, the goddess of love, and her followers perform elaborate rituals to honor her and seek her blessings in love. In China, the

Double Seventh Festival celebrates the annual meeting of two star-crossed lovers—Zhinü and Niulang—where people pray for love and happiness. In the Celtic lands, handfasting was a common practice where couples would bind their hands together as a symbol of their commitment, a practice that has seen a revival in modern times.

Folk magic, often passed down through oral traditions, has a special place in the annals of love magic. The use of love spells in folk traditions was often a blend of superstition, herbal knowledge, and the belief in the supernatural. Love magic was not always about finding new love; it was equally about protecting love from the evil eye, infidelity, or waning passion.

In the Renaissance, as occult knowledge spread with the printing press, grimoires containing love spells and incantations became more accessible. The era saw a fusion of hermeticism, alchemy, and astrology in the pursuit of love, with figures like Agrippa and John Dee contributing to the knowledge of esoteric love practices.

Today, love magic has taken on new forms, integrating ancient wisdom with modern psychological understanding. While the spells and practices have evolved, the intent remains the same—to influence the ethereal energies and manifest love in our lives. The New Age movement has seen a resurgence in crystal healing, tarot readings, and energy work, all aimed at enhancing romantic connections.

Understanding the historical and cultural context of love magic enriches our practice by connecting us to a lineage of human expression and spiritual pursuit. While the tools and methods may differ across time and geography, the essence of love magic remains a testament to our shared human experience—the longing for love, and the belief in magic to bring it within our grasp.

The Philosophy Behind Magical Practices in Love

As we delve into the realm of love magic, it is essential to understand the philosophical underpinnings that support and give meaning to these ancient practices. Love magic is not merely about the casting of spells or the creation of enchantments; it is rooted in a deeper philosophy that connects us to the very essence of human experience—love, connection, and the intertwining of souls.

Central to the philosophy of love magic is the Hermetic principle of correspondence, encapsulated in the adage "as above, so below; as within, so without." This principle suggests that the macrocosm and microcosm are reflections of one another, and that to influence one, we must understand and align with the other. In the context of love, this means that to attract love externally, one must first cultivate love internally, creating a harmony between one's personal energy and the energy one wishes to attract.

Intention is the cornerstone of any magical practice. It is the focused desire, the clear visualization, and the directed will that propels a spell or ritual into effectiveness. The philosophy of love magic holds that by setting a clear and positive intention, we align our personal will with the universal will, thereby manifesting our desires in the realm of love. This philosophy echoes through the story of Elena, who, through daily affirmations of self-love and worthiness, found her intentions reflected back to her in a loving and supportive partner.

The ethics of love magic are paramount. True love cannot be coerced or manipulated; therefore, love magic is not about controlling another's will or infringing upon their freedom. The philosophy here teaches respect for the sovereignty of each soul and the natural course of events. Love spells are designed to

attract love to us without specific targets, to enhance our own attractiveness, or to heal and strengthen existing relationships.

Sympathy, or sympathetic magic, operates on the premise that like attracts like. In love magic, this often involves using symbols, tokens, or actions that correspond to love, such as roses for passion, sugar for sweetness, or red for the heart's desires. These items and gestures are not magical in and of themselves, but when charged with intention, they become powerful tools for attracting love.

The philosophy also emphasizes the importance of cultivating one's personal energy. A vibrant and positive personal energy not only attracts love but also enriches it. This is seen in practices such as meditation, chakra balancing, and aura cleansing, which help maintain an energetically healthy state conducive to giving and receiving love.

Love magic recognizes the coexistence of fate and free will. While there may be certain predestined encounters in our lives, how we nurture and develop these connections is a matter of personal choice. The philosophy encourages us to use love magic to open the doors to potential love but also to actively engage in the relationship with attention and care.

The philosophy behind magical practices in love is profound and multi-faceted. It invites us to engage with love magic in a way that is respectful, ethical, and aligned with the highest good of all involved. By understanding these philosophical principles, we gain insight into not only how to perform love magic but why it works, providing us with a deeper connection to the magic we weave in our pursuit of love.

Chapter 2: Preparing the Self for Magical Love

Self-Love as the Foundation for Relationship Magic

Before one can manifest love in the external world, one must first cultivate it within. This is the cardinal rule in the realm of magical practices for achieving love. Self-love is not merely a state of feeling good about oneself; it is a profound recognition and acceptance of one's worth and a commitment to one's well-being. It is from this nurturing soil that the seed of external love finds the strength to grow.

Self-love begins with self-reflection. Like the moon reflecting the sun's light, we must reflect upon our inner selves to understand our true worth. This reflective process can be enhanced through meditation, journaling, and other introspective practices that allow us to confront and heal our inner wounds. Through this, we become aware of the narratives we carry about ourselves and can begin to rewrite those that do not serve our highest good.

Harmony within oneself is essential for harmony in a relationship. Magical practices such as chakra alignments or affirmations can be utilized to create inner balance. When we are harmonious within, we are more likely to attract and maintain relationships that are harmonious too. For instance, when Sophia began a daily practice of heart chakra meditations, she found that not only did her self-esteem improve, but her relationships became more nurturing and less conflictual.

Creating rituals for self-love can have a profound impact on how we view ourselves and, subsequently, how others view us. This can be as simple as a ritual bath infused with rose petals and salts for purification and love, or a more elaborate ritual involving anointing oneself with oils and reciting affirmations of self-worth.

Acceptance is a key component of self-love. Through acceptance, we learn to love ourselves as we are, recognizing our imperfections as part of our unique magic. This acceptance can be fostered through spells that emphasize personal uniqueness and the releasing of self-judgment. As we grow in acceptance of ourselves, we set the stage for others to accept and love us in equal measure.

Boundaries are an expression of self-love. They communicate to ourselves and others what we find acceptable and what we do not. Magic can aid in setting these boundaries through the creation of protective amulets or through visualization exercises that shield one's energy from negativity.

Take the story of Marcus, who, through a daily ritual of looking at himself in the mirror and expressing love and appreciation for who he was, transformed his self-image and eventually found a partner who mirrored that love. Or consider Angela, who carried a self-love talisman that reminded her of her commitment to her well-being, leading to healthier relationship choices.

Self-love is the cornerstone upon which the magic of relationships is built. Without it, our spells and rituals are like seeds sown on barren land. With it, we create a fertile ground for love to flourish. By dedicating time and energy to the cultivation of self-love, we do the essential groundwork for attracting and nurturing the romantic love we desire. It is through self-love that we become our own magical match, ready to unite with another in a dance of mutually empowering love.

Cleansing and Purification Rituals for the Heart and Spirit

Before embarking on the journey to find or enhance love, it is crucial to clear the pathways of the heart and spirit. Just as we would tidy our homes before welcoming a cherished guest, so must we cleanse our emotional and spiritual domains to invite new or renewed love.

Our hearts and spirits can become cluttered with the residue of past hurts, disappointments, and negative patterns. These lingering energies can obstruct the flow of new love into our lives. Energetic hygiene through cleansing and purification rituals helps to release these blockages, creating a clean slate for love to write its next chapter.

One of the first steps in any cleansing ritual is the act of release. This can be symbolically achieved through the burning of written notes that contain past grievances, regrets, or fears. The smoke symbolizes the ascent of these burdens, leaving the heart lighter and free. For example, Michael wrote letters to all his past loves, expressing forgiveness and gratitude before burning them in a ceremonial fire, symbolizing the end of those emotional chapters and the readiness to begin anew.

Water is a powerful element for purification, universally used in rituals to cleanse both the body and spirit. Ritual baths can be particularly effective, especially when infused with salts for grounding and herbs like lavender for healing, or rose petals for opening the heart. Envision the water washing away all that no longer serves you, leaving behind a clear and open heart.

Smudging, the practice of burning sacred herbs like sage, palo santo, or sweetgrass, is used to cleanse a space or individual of negative or stagnant energy. Similarly, sound clearing with bells, chimes, or singing bowls can recalibrate the energy of a space or your personal aura, promoting a sense of peace and clarity.

The environment we inhabit plays a significant role in our energetic health. Creating a space that reflects purity, harmony, and tranquility can support the heart and spirit in maintaining a cleansed state. This might involve de-cluttering living spaces, setting up altars or areas of tranquility, and regularly refreshing the energy with natural light and fresh air.

In the pursuit of love, our inner landscape must be tended to with the same care as a gardener tends to their garden. The rituals of cleansing and purification help remove the weeds of old pains and the debris of past relationships, allowing new love to flourish. This chapter will guide you through several known rituals, providing detailed instructions on how to carry them out for a heart and spirit receptive to love.

Ritual Bathing for Emotional Release

Ritual bathing is a time-honored method for purifying the body and, by extension, the soul.

1. Ingredients: Gather sea salt, essential oils (like lavender for calming, rose for love, or jasmine for prosperity), herbs (such as rosemary for purification), and a piece of clear quartz to amplify intentions.

2. Preparation: Fill your bathtub with warm water, and as it runs, add in the sea salt, a few drops of your chosen essential oil, and herbs.

3. Bathing: Submerge yourself in the tub, close your eyes, and focus on your breath. Visualize the water drawing out negativity from your body and spirit, leaving you cleansed and refreshed.

4. Completion: Drain the tub and imagine all the negative energy flowing away. Step out, dry yourself, and hold the clear quartz, setting the intention for clear, open pathways to love.

Smudging to Clear the Aura

Smudging is a practice used by many indigenous cultures to cleanse a person or space of negative energies.

1. Materials: You'll need a smudge stick made of sage, cedar, or sweetgrass.

2. Process: Light the smudge stick and allow it to smolder. Gently wave the smoke around your body, starting at the head and moving down to the feet. As you do this, envision the smoke absorbing negativity and tension.

3. Invocation: Use an affirmation or prayer as you smudge, such as "With this smoke, I cleanse myself of all that does not serve me, and I open my heart to the love that awaits."

Sound Clearing with Bells or Singing Bowls

Sound vibrations can break up stagnant energy and promote a harmonious environment.

1. Instrument: Choose a clear-sounding bell or a singing bowl.

2. Practice: Ring the bell or play the bowl near your heart center and around your body, especially over areas that feel heavy or blocked.

3. Intention: With each sound wave, imagine your aura brightening and any darkness dissipating, leaving a light space for love.

Candle Ritual for Releasing the Past

Candles can be a focus for setting intentions and letting go of old emotional baggage.

1. Preparation: Choose a candle in a color that represents love to you, such as pink for affection or green for healing.

2. Ritual: Light the candle and write down on a piece of paper all the past hurts or issues you wish to release.

3. Action: Safely burn the paper in a fireproof bowl or container, allowing the candle's flame to transform your past pain into wisdom and learning.

4. Closing: As the paper turns to ash, affirm that you are free from these ties, and your heart is ready for new experiences of love.

Nature's Cleansing with Earth and Air

Engaging with the elements of nature can provide a powerful cleansing experience.

1. Earth: Find a quiet spot in nature, perhaps under a tree or by a body of water. Take off your shoes, and stand or sit directly on the ground. Imagine excess energy flowing out of you and into the Earth, which absorbs and neutralizes it.

2. Air: On a windy day, stand outside with your arms open and allow the wind to pass over and around you. With each gust, envision that the wind is carrying away any remnants of sadness or regret.

Herbal Pouches for Ongoing Purification

Herbal pouches, also known as medicine bags or spell bags, carry the ongoing intention for heart cleansing.

1. Creation: Choose herbs that resonate with love and purification such as lavender, rose petals, and chamomile. Place these in a small pouch along with a stone like rose quartz.

2. Activation: Hold the pouch in your hands, close your eyes, and visualize your heart chakra opening and expanding, free from past wounds.

3. Maintenance: Carry the pouch with you, sleep with it under your pillow, or place it on your altar as a reminder of your ongoing process of heart purification.

Each of these rituals serves to cleanse the heart and spirit, making them a fertile ground for the seeds of new love to take root. Remember, the key to these practices is your intention; focus your mind on what you wish to release and the love you wish to invite into your life as you perform these rituals, and the magic will follow.

Consider the story of Anna, who after a difficult breakup, created a weekly ritual of cleansing her home and aura, which helped her to let go of the past and embrace hope for new love. Or Jake, who found solace in nature, often taking walks in the forest where he performed grounding rituals, connecting with the earth to purify his intentions and open his heart to future relationships.

For some, fasting or following a detoxifying diet can serve as a physical parallel to spiritual cleansing, reinforcing the intention to rid oneself of past toxins—emotional and physical. This practice can sharpen the mind and reinvigorate the spirit, making it more receptive to love's vibrations.

Cleansing and purification rituals are essential preparations for the heart and spirit, akin to opening the windows of a long-closed room to let in light and air. They allow us to shed the old and welcome the new, ensuring that when love comes knocking, it finds a home that is ready, receptive, and resonant with the possibilities of magic and love.

Aligning with the Intention of True Love

The pursuit of true love is not merely a quest for a partner but a quest for alignment with the heart's deepest yearnings and the universe's expansive potential for connection. This alignment is a form of magic in itself, a conjuring of the highest order. True love vibrates at a frequency of authenticity, compassion, and selflessness. It is the resonance of soulmates and kindred spirits. Aligning with this frequency requires an understanding that true love is not found, but rather, it is cultivated both within oneself and in the space shared with another.

Setting the Intention

1. Clarity: Begin with a clear and focused mind. Understand what true love means to you beyond the superficial. Contemplate the qualities that embody such a love and how it would feel in your life.

2. Visualization: Envision the love you desire with all your senses. See the interaction, feel the connection, hear the words of love, and immerse yourself in this visualization with full emotional engagement.

3. Affirmation: Use affirmations to reinforce your intention. Repeat affirmations like "I am worthy of deep, true love, and I open myself to receive it in abundance" to solidify your resolve.

Rituals for Alignment

1. Candle Ritual: Light a pink candle for affection, a white candle for purity of intention, or a green candle for healing any barriers to love. As the candle burns, it symbolizes the illumination of your intention across the spiritual planes.

2. Crystal Grid: Create a crystal grid using stones associated with love, such as rose quartz for love, rhodonite for compassion, and emerald for unconditional love. Arrange them in a sacred geometric pattern to amplify their energies and your intention.

3. Herbal Sachets: Craft a sachet filled with herbs like basil for love, cinnamon for passion, and lavender for peace. Keep this sachet under your pillow, in your pocket, or in a special place to remind you of your alignment with the intention of true love.

Living in Alignment

1. Daily Practices: Incorporate small daily practices that reflect your intention for true love. It could be as simple as offering kindness to strangers or as personal as nurturing self-love.

2. Mindful Relationships: Engage in relationships mindfully, ensuring that your interactions with others reflect the true love you seek. This means practicing active listening, empathy, and open-hearted communication.

Consider the tale of Nora, who, after a series of unfulfilling relationships, began a nightly ritual of writing down the qualities she sought in a partner, and soon met a person who embodied these traits. Or Leo, who meditated daily on the feeling of love he desired, finding that his relationships began to deepen and reflect the love he had been cultivating within.

Alignment with true love is a journey, not a destination. It requires patience, as the universe works in its own time and ways. Trust that the love you are aligning with will manifest when the time is right.

Aligning with the intention of true love is an act of magical faith. It is a commitment to not only seek love but also to become a vessel for it. Through the practices and principles outlined in this chapter, you can fine-tune your heart's frequency to the vibration of true love and invite a profound connection into your life that is aligned with your highest intentions.

Exercises and Rituals to Cultivate Self-Love

In the alchemical process of attracting and nurturing love, the first and most crucial ingredient is self-love. It is the golden rule from which all magical practices draw their power. Without a deep, abiding love for oneself, the magic we seek in relationships with others can neither be fully appreciated nor sustained.

Affirmations are positive statements that, when repeated regularly, can reprogram our subconscious mind, reinforcing our self-worth and love.

1. Crafting Affirmations: Write affirmations that resonate with your personal journey towards self-love. Examples include "I am worthy of love and joy" or "I accept myself unconditionally."

2. Practicing Affirmations: Recite your affirmations each morning upon waking and each night before sleeping. Speak them in front of a mirror, looking into your own eyes to deepen the connection.

The Mirror Work Ritual

Mirror work is a powerful technique for building self-love, as it confronts us with our own gaze, which can be both challenging and transformative.

1. Setup: Stand or sit comfortably in front of a mirror in a quiet space where you will not be disturbed.

2. Process: Look into your eyes in the mirror and offer words of love and encouragement to yourself. You might start with "I love you" and then move on to more specific praises or affirmations.

3. Duration: Spend at least five minutes on this exercise, gradually increasing the time as you become more comfortable with the practice.

Self-Love Meditation

Meditation can quiet the mind and open the heart, allowing us to experience self-love on a deep, intuitive level.

1. Preparation: Find a quiet space where you can sit or lie down without interruption. You may light a candle or incense to create a serene atmosphere.

2. Meditation: Close your eyes and begin to breathe deeply. With each inhale, visualize love in the form of a warm light filling your body. With each exhale, release any self-criticism or doubt.

3. Focus: Direct your attention to your heart chakra, located in the center of your chest. Envision it glowing with a beautiful, soothing light, expanding with each breath.

The Gratitude Journal

Gratitude is a potent tool for cultivating self-love, as it shifts the focus from what we lack to the abundance that already exists within us.

1. Journaling: Keep a journal specifically for noting things you are grateful for about yourself—qualities, achievements, or even challenges you've overcome.

2. Daily Practice: Each day, write down at least three things that you are thankful for about yourself. Reflect on these and allow yourself to feel the gratitude fully.

Rituals of Self-Care

Self-care rituals are tangible acts of self-love that nourish the body, mind, and soul.

1. Activities: Engage in activities that you enjoy and that make you feel good about yourself. This could be a hobby, exercise, a spa day, or simply a quiet hour with a book.

2. Consistency: Make these activities a regular part of your routine to reinforce the importance of caring for yourself.

Emma, for instance, found that her morning ritual of yoga and positive affirmations helped her cultivate a stronger sense of self-love. Daniel discovered that by writing in his gratitude journal every evening, he was able to sleep with a sense of self-appreciation that had eluded him for years.

The journey to self-love is unique for each individual, but the destination is the same—a place where we value ourselves as deserving of all the love and magic life has to offer. By incorporating these exercises and rituals into our daily lives, we build a reservoir of self-love that not only empowers our magical practices but also brings us closer to the love we seek from others.

Chapter 3: The Basics of Magical Practice

A Beginner's Guide to Magic and Its Principles

Magic is an ancient art, a practice that transcends cultures and epochs, and at its core, it is about connecting with the energies of the universe to bring about change. For those beginning their magical journey, especially in the realm of love, understanding its foundational principles is crucial.

Magic, in its simplest form, is the art of influencing the material and ethereal worlds through will, intent, and the manipulation of energy. It is based on the belief that everything in the universe is interconnected, and thus, actions performed with focused intention can ripple out and effect change.

The principle of correspondence, a cornerstone of magical theory, posits that the microcosm reflects the macrocosm and that by influencing one, you can affect the other. In love magic, this means that personal transformations and inner work can manifest as changes in your romantic life.

Another fundamental principle is that of cause and effect. In magic, it is believed that every action has a reaction, and this extends to the metaphysical realm. Thus, when casting love spells, it is crucial to consider the potential effects, not only on yourself but on others as well, and to approach the practice with respect and responsibility.

Intention is the driving force behind magic. It is important to be clear about what you want to achieve. This clarity will direct the energy of your work and determine its effectiveness. Intentions in love magic should be focused on attracting love in its most beneficial form rather than targeting a specific individual, which can infringe upon their free will.

Practicing magic often requires creating a sacred space—a physical or metaphysical area where you can focus your will and energy. This could be an altar, a room, or even a corner of your home dedicated to your magical work. It should be a place where you can meditate, cast spells, and perform rituals without interruption.

Rituals are structured ceremonies that incorporate specific tools to direct energy and manifest intentions. Common tools in love magic include:

- Candles: Different colors can represent various aspects of love, with red for passion, pink for romance, and green for healing.

- Crystals: Stones like rose quartz for unconditional love or amethyst for spiritual connection can amplify your intentions.

- Herbs: Plants like lavender for peace in love and basil for harmony are often used in spells and potions.

Spellcasting is a practical application of magical principles. It involves gathering materials, reciting words of power, and visualizing your intentions. The most effective spells are those you create yourself, as they carry your personal energy and intent.

James, new to the practice of magic, began by setting up a small altar where he would meditate on love each morning. He found that the simple act of lighting a candle and focusing on his intention for love each day began to open his heart in unexpected ways.

Maria crafted a love spell using rose petals and a piece of rose quartz. She performed her spell during the full moon, a time when magical energies are believed to be at their peak. Over the following months, she noticed a shift in her romantic encounters, aligning more closely with her intentions.

How to Set Intentions and Choose the Right Magical Methods for Love

Setting intentions is akin to plotting a course on a map before embarking on a journey. In magic, especially when it revolves around love, having a clear and focused intention is vital. Intentions are the seeds from which the flowers of outcome bloom. They are not just wishes; they are commitments to ourselves and the universe about what we desire to manifest.

1. Clarity: Begin with a clear vision of what you want in a relationship. Is it companionship, passion, stability, or growth? Visualize the relationship you aspire to create.

2. Specificity: General intentions can yield unfocused results. Be as specific as possible with your intentions without infringing on anyone's free will. For instance, rather than intending to make a certain person love you, intend to attract a loving and mutually fulfilling relationship.

There are countless magical practices, and selecting the right one for your intention is crucial.

1. Alignment with Intentions: Choose methods that align with the nature of your intention. If you seek passionate love, a spell involving red candles or spicy herbs may be appropriate. For gentle love, pink candles and sweet scents like rose might be more fitting.

2. Cultural Resonance: Be mindful of cultural practices and choose methods that resonate with your beliefs and background. This ensures your energy aligns with the practice authentically.

3. Practicality and Accessibility: The method you choose should be practical for you to perform and within your means. If a ritual requires a rare herb that is not accessible to you, it's better to find an alternative that you can obtain easily.

Rituals and Spells for Setting Intentions

1. New Moon Ritual: The new moon is a time for setting intentions. Write your love intention on a piece of paper, light a pink candle, and meditate on your intention. When you feel ready, burn the paper safely in the candle flame, releasing your intention to the universe.

2. Love Intention Jar: Create an intention jar filled with symbols of love: rose petals, heart-shaped stones, or anything that represents love to you. Seal your intention inside and place the jar on your altar or in a special place.

3. Visualization and Meditation: Daily visualization strengthens your intention. Sit quietly, breathing deeply, and create a vivid mental image of the love you wish to attract. Feel the emotions that come with this love as if it's already part of your life.

Emma set an intention to find self-love and completed a ritual bath every week, each time affirming her worthiness of love. Six months into her practice, she met a partner who reflected the love she had cultivated within herself.

Tom created a love sigil, a magical symbol, to represent his intention to find a partner who shared his passion for adventure. He carried this sigil with him on travels, and it was on one of these journeys that he met his significant other.

Setting a clear, well-defined intention is the cornerstone of any successful magical practice. By aligning your desires with the appropriate rituals and methods, you create a powerful synergy that can significantly enhance your prospects in love. Remember, the magic of intention is potent; wield it with wisdom, and it will serve as a beacon, attracting the love you seek into your life.

Tools and Symbols Commonly Used in Love Magic and Creating Sacred Space for Magical Work

For the practitioner of love magic, certain tools and symbols have stood the test of time, imbued with the power to attract, nurture, and protect love. Moreover, the space in which one conducts magical work is of equal importance—a sacred space amplifies the energies and intentions at play.

Tools of Love Magic

1. Candles: The flame of a candle is a powerful symbol of the light of love. Pink candles are used to attract romance, red for passionate love, and white for pure, unconditional love. Each candle lit is a beacon calling to the heart's desires.

2. Crystals and Stones: Crystals such as rose quartz are synonymous with love magic, known for their ability to open and heal the heart. Rhodonite promotes forgiveness, while emerald fosters loyalty and successful partnerships.

3. Herbs and Plants: Lavender can be used to calm turbulent emotions, basil to foster harmony, and roses for all matters of the heart. These can be used in spells, worn, or placed around your sacred space.

4. Incense and Oils: The smoke of incense can carry your intentions to the heavens. Scents like vanilla, jasmine, and ylang-ylang are powerful allies in love magic. Similarly, anointing oils can be used on the body or candles to draw in love.

5. Sigils and Symbols: The creation of sigils, which are symbols designed for a specific magical purpose, can be particularly powerful. The heart symbol, the Venus sign (♀), and the infinity loop are potent symbols for love spells and rituals.

6. Tarot Cards and Divination Tools: The Lovers card, Two of Cups, and the Empress are often used in love readings and can also be incorporated into spells as representations of the relationship you seek to manifest or nurture.

Creating a Sacred Space

1. Choosing Your Space: Your sacred space should be a place where you feel at ease and free from interruption. It may be a corner of your bedroom, a private nook, or even a portable box that holds your magical tools and can be set up wherever you go.

2. Cleansing the Space: Before consecrating your space, cleanse it using smudging, aspersing with saltwater, or sound clearing with bells or singing bowls. This removes any negative or stagnant energy and prepares the space for sacred work.

3. Consecration: Consecrate your space by calling in the four elements, the cardinal directions, or any deities or spirits you work with. Set the intention that this space is protected and sacred.

4. Altar Setup: An altar can be a focal point of your sacred space. Adorn it with symbols of love, your magical tools, and any offerings or representations of the divine.

5. Maintaining Your Space: Keep your sacred space clean and tidy. Regularly refresh the energies by rearranging the items, lighting new candles, and offering fresh intentions.

The tools and symbols of love magic serve as extensions of your intentions, each adding its unique energy to your spells and rituals. Combined with a sacred space dedicated to your magical work, these tools create a powerful matrix for love magic to thrive. Whether you are a seasoned practitioner or just beginning your magical journey, understanding and utilizing these tools, symbols, and spaces will enhance your ability to weave love into the fabric of your reality.

Part II: Attracting Love

Chapter 4: Preparing for New Love

Clearing Past Energies and Emotional Baggage

Before one can fully embrace the potential of new love, it is essential to address and clear the lingering energies of past relationships and the emotional baggage they may have left behind. Holding onto these remnants can create blockages that inadvertently repel the love we seek.

Emotional baggage is the accumulation of unresolved feelings, disappointments, traumas, and heartbreak from past relationships. It can manifest as patterns of behavior, unconscious fears, or a general reluctance to open up to new connections.

The first step in clearing past energies is to recognize their presence and influence on your current life. This can be done through self-reflection, journaling, or even through tarot readings that focus on your emotional state.

Rituals for Releasing Past Bonds

1. **Cord-Cutting Ceremony**: The cord-cutting ceremony is a symbolic act meant to energetically sever the ties with someone from your past with whom you've had an emotional relationship. It's important to note that this ritual is not about erasing memories or undoing experiences; it's about reclaiming your personal energy and allowing for healing to take place.

Preparation:

1. Timing: Choose a time when you will not be disturbed. Some prefer to align the ritual with a waning moon, as it symbolizes letting go and release.

2. Setting the Space: Create a quiet, sacred space where you can perform the ritual without interruptions. This could be at your altar or any space where you feel safe and at peace.

3. Tools and Symbols: Gather a piece of string or ribbon to represent the cord, a pair of scissors or a ritual knife (athame) for cutting, a candle, and any other items you feel drawn to include, such as crystals or photographs.

The Ceremony:

1. Centering: Begin by centering yourself. Take deep breaths, meditate for a few moments, or do whatever grounding exercises work for you.

2. Invoking Protection: Call upon any deities, guides, or guardians you work with for protection and support. Visualize yourself surrounded by a white light that safeguards your energy during the ritual.

3. Cord Visualization: Light the candle and focus on the flame. Visualize the cord that ties you to the person from your past. It may appear as a rope, chain, or thread. See it as extending from your solar plexus or heart chakra to the other person.

4. Affirmation of Intent: Speak your intention aloud. It can be something like, "I hereby sever any cords of attachment that no longer serve my highest good, with love and gratitude for the lessons learned."

5. Cutting the Cord: Take the string or ribbon and say, "This represents the cord between [name] and me." Hold the string taut between your hands. Then, with the scissors or athame, cut the string while visualizing the energetic cord being severed. As you cut the string, you might say, "I cut this cord and release its hold on me."

6. Healing Visualization: After cutting the cord, visualize the ends of the severed cord being sealed with light, preventing energy from flowing away from you.

Imagine a warm, healing light filling any voids left by the cutting, bringing peace and healing to your heart.

7. Closure: Allow the candle to burn down safely. Collect the pieces of the cut string and any other ritual items. You may choose to bury them, throw them in a natural body of water, or dispose of them in a way that signifies release and completion for you.

8. Aftercare: Take time to nurture yourself after the ceremony. You may feel a range of emotions, and it's important to be gentle with yourself. Drink water, rest, or take a salt bath to further cleanse your energy.

Jessica had been holding onto feelings for her ex-partner, Tom, and felt this was blocking her from moving on. She decided to perform a cord-cutting ceremony during the waning moon. In the quiet of her room, with candles lit and a piece of string representing her attachment to Tom, she followed the steps of the ceremony. After cutting the string, she felt an immediate sense of lightness and freedom. In the weeks following, Jessica noticed that her thoughts were less and less occupied with memories of Tom, and she felt more open to new possibilities in love.

2. **Burning Letters**: The Burning Letters Ritual is a cathartic exercise that allows you to release the emotional hold of past relationships, grievances, or self-limiting beliefs. It's a symbolic way to let go of old baggage and can be particularly healing. Here's how to carry out the ritual with specific steps:

Preparation:

1. Materials Needed: Paper and a pen; A fireproof container or a fireplace; Matches or a lighter; Optional items for ambiance: candles, calming music, crystals, or incense.

2. Choosing the Right Time:

- Similar to the cord-cutting ceremony, many prefer to conduct this ritual during a waning moon as it symbolizes release and letting go.

- Ensure you have enough time for the ritual without feeling rushed.

The Ritual:

1. Writing the Letters:

   - Write letters to those you wish to release from your emotional space. This could be past lovers, friends, family members, or even aspects of yourself.

   - Express all your feelings, regrets, wishes, and the reasons why you need to let go. Be honest and thorough; this is for your eyes only.

   - If you're addressing personal traits or past events, write them down as if they were entities you're communicating with.

2. Creating a Safe Space:

   - Clear a space where you can perform the ritual without disturbance.

   - If you're using candles, light them now to create a sacred ambiance.

   - Open windows or ensure good ventilation for the smoke to escape.

3. The Burning:

   - Once you have written all you need to, fold the letters and hold them over the fireproof container.

   - As you light them, you might say something like, "With this flame, I release what no longer serves me. I let go of the past and welcome new beginnings."

   - Place the burning letters in the container and watch them turn to ash. As the paper burns, envision the emotional ties burning away as well.

4. Reflection and Release:

- As the fire dies down, spend a few moments in reflection. Acknowledge the release of these emotions and affirm your readiness to move forward.

- If you used additional items like crystals or wrote additional notes, you could cleanse them with smoke or saltwater to symbolically cleanse their energy as well.

5. Disposal of the Ashes:

- Once the ashes have cooled, you can bury them outside, scatter them to the wind, or flush them down running water, symbolizing a final release.

- Some prefer to scatter ashes in a place that holds significance to the past relationship or situation.

David felt burdened by the resentment he held towards his former business partner, which also seemed to affect his trust in new relationships. He decided to perform the Burning Letters Ritual, writing a detailed letter where he poured out his feelings of betrayal and disappointment. After burning the letter, David felt a profound sense of relief and found himself more open to trusting again, both in his professional and personal life.

3. **Bath Rituals**: Bath rituals harness the natural cleansing properties of water, combined with various elements like salts, herbs, and essential oils, to facilitate emotional and spiritual purification. Here's a step-by-step guide on how to perform a bath ritual for releasing emotional baggage and past energies:

Preparation:

1. Materials Needed:

- Epsom or sea salt for purification.

- Essential oils such as lavender for relaxation, rose for love and healing, or eucalyptus for clearing negative energy.

- Herbs or flowers like rose petals for love, chamomile for soothing, or sage for cleansing.

- Crystals such as rose quartz for self-love or amethyst for emotional healing (optional).

- Candles and soothing music to set a serene atmosphere.

2. Timing:

- Choose a time when you will not be disturbed, perhaps during the evening to help you unwind and process the release as you sleep.

The Ritual:

1. Setting the Space:

- Begin by cleaning your bathtub to ensure physical and energetic cleanliness.

- Fill your tub with warm water, adjusting the temperature to your comfort level.

- As the tub fills, add the salts, a few drops of essential oils, and herbs or flower petals.

2. Charging the Bath:

- Hold your hands over the water and set your intention. You might say, "I cleanse myself of past hurts and open my heart to new beginnings."

- If using crystals, place them around the edge of the tub or in the water, ensuring they are water-safe.

3. Creating Ambiance:
   - Light candles around the bath and play soothing music to help shift your energy into a meditative state.

4. Entering the Bath:
   - Step into the bath slowly, acclimating to the warmth and feeling of the water.
   - Submerge yourself as much as possible, closing your eyes, and focusing on your breath.

5. The Release:
   - Visualize the water drawing out the negative energies, past memories, and emotional blocks from your body.
   - With each exhale, imagine releasing these energies into the water, where they are neutralized and dissolved.

6. Affirmations and Meditation:
   - Recite affirmations that resonate with the release and healing you're seeking, such as "With every breath, I release the past and nourish my spirit with love."
   - You can meditate, pray, or simply soak in silence, allowing your mind to clear.

7. Completing the Ritual:
   - Once you feel the release is complete, stand up slowly and let the water drain from the tub.
   - Visualize that as the water spirals down the drain, it carries away all that you've released.
   - Step out of the tub and gently towel yourself off. It's important to do this lovingly, as a form of self-care.

8. Aftercare:

- Drink plenty of water after the bath to rehydrate and aid in the detoxification process.

- You may want to rest or sleep immediately after the bath to integrate the experience.

Samantha was dealing with the aftermath of a challenging breakup. She felt heavy with unresolved emotions and sought a way to cleanse herself of this burden. She prepared a bath ritual, adding Epsom salts, rose petals, and lavender oil to the water. As she soaked, she visualized her pain and sorrow dissolving away. When she emerged from the water, she felt a significant emotional shift, lighter and ready to heal and move forward.

Certain crystals can aid in the process of emotional healing and release. Black tourmaline, for example, is known for its protective and grounding properties, helping to clear negative energies. Rose quartz can aid in healing the heart chakra and encouraging self-love.

Forgiveness, both of oneself and others, is a potent form of emotional release. It does not excuse the past but frees you from being tethered to it. Forgiveness can be affirmed through meditation, prayer, or ritual, and it often requires repeated practice.

After the initial clearing, maintaining an environment free of past energies is essential. Regularly cleanse your living space, perform grounding and centering exercises, and meditate with crystals to ensure that old emotional energies do not reaccumulate.

Engaging with energy healing practices such as Reiki, acupuncture, or sound therapy can also be instrumental in releasing past emotional baggage. These modalities help to balance the energy centers in the body and promote emotional well-being.

Rituals for Opening the Heart to New Love

Embarking on a journey to find new love requires an open heart—one that is ready to give and receive affection. However, life's trials and past hurts can cause us to guard our hearts closely. To attract new love, it is essential to perform rituals that gently encourage our hearts to open again.

A welcoming heart space is an emotional and energetic environment where love is invited to enter. It's crucial to cultivate this space within ourselves before we can expect to find it in another.

Ritual 1: Heart Chakra Meditation

1. Setup: Find a quiet, comfortable place where you can sit without interruptions. You may choose to sit on a cushion or directly on the ground to feel more connected to the earth.

2. Process: Close your eyes and take deep breaths. Place your hands over your heart. Visualize a green or pink light glowing in your chest, growing warmer and brighter with each breath.

3. Affirmation: As you meditate, repeat affirmations that resonate with heart-opening, such as, "I open my heart to give and receive love freely and joyfully."

4. Duration: Continue this meditation for at least 10 minutes, allowing the energy of the heart chakra to expand and envelop you.

Ritual 2: Rose Quartz Crystal Work

1. Selection: Choose a rose quartz crystal, known for its properties of unconditional love and heart healing.

2. Cleansing: Cleanse the crystal by holding it under running water, placing it in moonlight, or smudging with sage.

3. Activation: Hold the rose quartz in your hands and set the intention to open your heart to new love. You might say, "With this crystal, I align my heart to the vibration of love."

4. Use: Carry the crystal with you, sleep with it under your pillow, or meditate with it to reinforce the heart-opening energy.

Ritual 3: Love Attraction Anointing Oil

1. Ingredients: Create an anointing oil using essential oils associated with love, such as rose, ylang-ylang, or jasmine. Dilute with a carrier oil like almond or jojoba.

2. Consecration: Bless the oil by holding it in your hands and stating your intention to attract love. You might recite, "This oil is charged with the magnetic energy of love."

3. Application: Anoint your heart area, wrists, and neck with the oil while visualizing your aura attracting love.

Ritual 4: Candle Magic for New Beginnings

1. Candle Selection: Choose a new candle, preferably pink or green, to symbolize love and the heart chakra.

2. Carving and Dressing: Carve symbols of love on the candle, such as hearts or your initials. Dress the candle with your love attraction anointing oil.

3. Lighting the Candle: Light the candle while focusing on your intention to open your heart to new love. You might recite a poem, a prayer, or simply speak from the heart about your readiness for love.

4. Visualization: As the candle burns, visualize your life filled with the love you desire. Imagine being with a new partner, feeling happy, secure, and loved.

Ritual 5: Creating a Love Altar

1. Space: Dedicate a space in your home as your love altar. This can be a shelf, a section of your nightstand, or a small table.

2. Objects: Place items that represent love to you on the altar. These can include fresh flowers, love letters written to your future partner, or images of couples in loving embraces.

3. Activation: Spend time at your altar daily, affirming your openness to new love and visualizing your life with your future partner.

After a period of isolation, Lucas decided it was time to open his heart again. He performed the candle magic ritual, lighting a pink candle each night while visualizing love entering his life. Within months, he found himself forming deep, meaningful connections, one of which blossomed into a loving relationship.

Chapter 5: The Art of Love Spells

An Introduction to Love Spells and Their Purpose

In the realm of magical practices, love spells are among the most sought-after rites. These enchantments are designed to draw love into one's life, enhance existing connections, or even heal a broken heart.

The Essence of Love Spells. At their core, love spells are about intention and the direction of energy to manifest a desired outcome in the area of love and relationships. They are not about subjugating another's will or bending the laws of free will but rather about aligning the energies of love and desire with the spell caster's own aura.

Types of Love Spells

1. Attraction Spells: These spells are intended to attract love to you. They are general in nature and do not target anyone specific but open the channels of love in your life.

2. Commitment Spells: Aimed at deepening the bonds of an existing relationship, these spells help foster a deeper connection and a commitment from a partner.

3. Healing Spells: Designed to heal emotional wounds, these spells can help one move past heartache and prepare for new love.

4. Self-Love Spells: Perhaps the most critical spells, these focus on enhancing one's self-esteem and capacity for self-love, which is the foundation of any successful relationship.

The purpose of love spells goes beyond the mere act of attracting a partner. They are rituals that serve to:

1. Clarify Desires: Casting a love spell requires clear understanding and articulation of what you seek in a relationship.

2. Release Blocks: Love spells can help to uncover and release emotional blockages that are preventing you from experiencing love.

3. Align Energy: They are tools to align your personal energy with the vibrational frequency of love, making you a magnet for affection and connection.

4. Foster Growth: By focusing on self-improvement and the cultivation of positive traits, love spells can encourage personal growth.

When conducting a love spell, there are several important considerations:

1. Timing: Many practitioners align their spells with lunar phases, casting spells on a new moon for new beginnings or a full moon for manifestation.

2. Materials: Common materials include candles, crystals, oils, and herbs, each with their own symbolic significance.

3. Visualization: A key component is the mental visualization of the desired outcome. Strong, clear imagery can help direct your intent.

4. Words of Power: Spells often include chants, mantras, or affirmations that are repeated to raise energy and solidify intent.

Step-by-Step Guides for Simple Love Spells

Love spells can range from complex rituals to simple, heartfelt enchantments. For those beginning their magical journey or preferring a more straightforward approach, simple love spells can be just as effective. In this chapter, we present step-by-step guides to performing easy yet potent love spells.

Spell 1: Candle Love Spell

Candles are a staple in love magic due to their symbolism of light, warmth, and transformation.

Materials: One pink candle (for romance) or red candle (for passion); A piece of paper and a pen; Rose oil or your favorite essential oil; Matches or a lighter.

Steps:

1. Set Your Space: Find a quiet place where you won't be interrupted. Cleanse the area if desired, using incense or sage.

2. Prepare the Candle: Carve your initials (or a symbol of love like a heart) into the candle. Anoint it with rose oil, moving from the base to the wick to draw love toward you.

3. Write Your Intentions: On the piece of paper, write down the qualities you desire in a romantic partner or the feelings you wish to experience in your love life.

4. Light the Candle: Place the paper under the candle holder. Focus on your intentions as you light the candle. Watch the flame for a few moments, visualizing your desires coming to life.

5. Meditate and Visualize: Spend 5-10 minutes meditating on the warm glow of the candle. Picture your life filled with the love you seek.

6. Close the Spell: Once you feel ready, blow out the candle or let it burn down safely. Thank the universe for hearing your request.

Spell 2: Rose Quartz and Lavender Love Attraction Sachet

Rose quartz is known as the stone of love, and lavender is praised for its calming properties and ability to attract love.

Materials: A small piece of rose quartz; Dried lavender flowers; Pink or white sachet bag; Pink ribbon.

Steps:

1. Charge the Rose Quartz: Hold the stone in your hands, envisioning it being filled with loving energy. Set the intention that this stone will attract the love you desire.

2. Prepare the Sachet: Fill the sachet bag with dried lavender flowers and place the charged rose quartz inside.

3. Seal the Sachet: Tie the bag with a pink ribbon, making three knots. With each knot, affirm your intention to find love.

4. Place the Sachet: Keep the sachet under your pillow, in your purse, or in a drawer where you store your clothes, especially undergarments, to surround yourself with the energy of love.

Spell 3: Love Affirmation Ritual

Affirmations are powerful tools for manifesting desires and can be used effectively in love spells.

Materials: A quiet space; A list of love affirmations.

Steps:

1. Write Your Affirmations: Create affirmations that resonate with your quest for love. For example, "I am worthy of a loving, joyful relationship."

2. Relax and Center: Sit in a comfortable position, breathe deeply, and achieve a state of relaxation.

3. Recite Your Affirmations: Speak your affirmations aloud with conviction and belief. Visualize each one as a truth manifesting in your life.

4. Repeat Regularly: Commit to reciting your affirmations daily, ideally in the morning upon waking and at night before sleeping.

Detailed Guide on Love-Attracting Spells

Love-attracting spells are designed to draw romantic energies toward you, creating an aura that beckons new or deeper love into your life. These spells are not about ensnaring a particular person's will or affection. Instead, they're about enhancing your own energetic allure, making you a beacon for love. The key is to work with your intentions, the natural elements, and symbolic items to invite the essence of love into your existence.

Spell 1: The Honey Jar Spell for Sweet Love

A honey jar spell is a traditional folk magic spell that sweetens your energy, making you more attractive to love.

Materials: A small glass jar with a lid; Honey; Rose petals or dried roses; Lavender buds; Basil for fidelity; A pink or red candle; A piece of paper and a pen.

Steps:

1. Prepare Your Intentions: Write down what you're looking for in love on the piece of paper. Be specific about the qualities you desire in a relationship, not a specific person.

2. Assemble the Jar: Place the rose petals, lavender, and basil inside the jar. As you add each ingredient, focus on the quality it represents.

3. Add the Honey: Pour honey over the herbs and paper, filling the jar while visualizing love filling your life.

4. Seal the Jar: Close the jar tightly. Hold it in your hands and warm it with your energy as you recite your intentions.

5. Candle Sealing: Light the candle and drip its wax onto the jar lid to seal it, reaffirming your intentions for love.

6. Maintain the Spell: Place the jar on your altar or a special place. Light a candle on top of it once a week to reinforce your intentions.

Spell 2: The Attraction Sigil

Sigils are magical symbols created for a specific purpose, in this case, to attract love.

Materials: A piece of paper and a pen; Your focus and creativity.

Steps:

1. Craft Your Sigil: Write out your intention, such as "I attract love easily." Remove vowels and duplicate letters, then combine the remaining letters into a symbol that resonates with you.

2. Charge Your Sigil: Focus on the sigil, meditate on it, or pass it through the smoke of incense, asking the universe to charge it with energy.

3. Release Your Intentions: Burn the sigil, bury it, or place it somewhere special. Trust that the sigil is releasing your intentions to the universe.

Spell 3: Love Drawing Bath

Water is a powerful conduit for energy, and a ritual bath can help cleanse away blocks to love and draw in new romance.

Materials: Epsom or sea salts; Rose petals or essential oil; A cleansed and charged rose quartz crystal; Candles and soft music.

Steps:

1. Prepare Your Bath: Fill your tub with warm water. Add the salts and a few drops of rose oil or petals as the water runs.

2. Set the Scene: Light candles and play music that evokes feelings of love and relaxation.

3. Enter the Bath: Step into the bath, holding the rose quartz. Submerge as much as possible, relaxing into the warmth.

4. Visualize: Close your eyes and imagine love energies swirling around you, infusing your aura with attractiveness and charm.

5. Finish the Ritual: Drain the tub and visualize all obstacles to love leaving your body and life with the water.

Customizing Spells for Individual Needs

When it comes to matters of the heart, a one-size-fits-all approach rarely suffices. Each individual's journey to love is unique, filled with personal dreams, challenges, and circumstances. Customizing your love spells allows you to address your specific desires and obstacles, making your magical practice more personally meaningful and effective.

Before customizing a spell, it's crucial to have a deep understanding of what you truly need in your love life. Reflect on past relationships, your current situation, and your desires for the future. Consider what has worked for you and what hasn't, and the qualities you seek in a partner and relationship.

Steps for Customizing Spells

1. Set Clear Intentions: Your intention is the driving force of your spell. Be precise about what you want to attract, heal, or enhance in your love life.

2. Select Corresponding Elements: Choose herbs, crystals, candles, and colors that correspond to your specific love intentions. For example, use rose quartz for unconditional love, red candles for passion, or jasmine for spiritual connections.

3. Timing Your Spell: Align your spell with lunar phases, days of the week, or astrological timings that resonate with your love needs. New moons can be ideal for new beginnings in love, while Fridays, ruled by Venus, are perfect for spells related to romance.

4. Crafting Your Rituals: Modify the structure of spells to fit your life. If you have a busy schedule, a simple but consistent ritual may work best. If you enjoy elaborate magic, you might incorporate more complex ceremonies.

5. Personalizing Your Chants and Affirmations: Write your own chants, poems, or affirmations that speak directly to your heart and situation.

6. Incorporating Personal Symbols: Use symbols that are meaningful to you, such as a piece of jewelry given to you by a loved one or an image that inspires feelings of love.

Examples of Customized Spells

1. For Healing a Broken Heart: If you're healing from a past relationship, create a ritual bath with sea salt for cleansing, add blue or green candles for healing, and choose a comforting herb like chamomile. Write a letter to your past self or relationship, then dissolve it in the bathwater as a symbol of letting go.

2. To Attract a New Love: If you're looking to attract new love, consider crafting a vision board that represents your desires. Use a pink candle for gentle love or a red candle for fiery passion, placing it at the center of your board. Surround it with images and objects that represent the love you seek.

3. For Deepening an Existing Relationship: If your aim is to deepen the connection with your current partner, create a spell jar with both of your hair strands, add honey to sweeten the relationship, and place rose petals for romance. Seal it with wax from a candle you both have held, signifying your joined intentions.

Tailoring spells to your individual needs not only enhances their effectiveness but also deepens your connection to the magical process. By taking the time to understand your desires and thoughtfully selecting each element of your spell, you craft a personalized magical work that resonates with your unique path to love. Remember, the magic is most potent when it's intimately yours.

Chapter 6: Enchantments and Charms

How to Create and Charge Talismans and Amulets for Love

Talismans and amulets have been used for centuries as objects of power, protection, and transformation. In love magic, these objects are charged with specific intentions to attract, nurture, or protect love.

The terms 'talisman' and 'amulet' are often used interchangeably, but traditionally, a talisman is an object charged with magical power to bring something to the bearer, while an amulet is meant to protect against specific dangers or negative influences. In the context of love, a talisman might be charged to attract love, while an amulet would protect one's heart against potential heartbreak.

Creating Your Love Talisman or Amulet

1. Selecting Your Object: Choose an object that resonates with love for you. This could be a piece of jewelry, a stone like rose quartz, a written love symbol, or any item you feel drawn to.

2. Cleansing Your Object: Before charging your talisman or amulet, cleanse it of any previous energy. This can be done by smudging with sage, burying it in salt, placing it in sunlight or moonlight, or using sound like a bell or singing bowl.

3. Consecrating Your Object: Dedicate your object to its purpose. You can do this by holding it in your hand, stating its purpose, and calling on any deities, spirits, or elements you work with to bless it.

Charging Your Talisman or Amulet

1. Charging by Moonlight: Place your talisman or amulet under the moonlight, preferably during a New Moon for new beginnings, or a Full Moon for bringing things to fruition. Leave it overnight to absorb the moon's energy.

2. Charging with Visualization: Hold your object in your hands and visualize it glowing with the energy of love. Picture the object attracting or exuding the love you desire.

3. Charging with Elements: You can also charge your talisman or amulet with the elements by burying it in the earth, passing it through candle flame, rinsing it with water, or blowing on it with your breath.

4. Charging with Intentions: Speak or write your intentions and place them with your talisman or amulet. You can write on paper and fold it around the object or simply recite your intentions while holding the object.

Activating Your Talisman or Amulet

1. Activation Ritual: Perform a simple activation ritual where you formally state the object's purpose. For example, "I activate this talisman to attract true love into my life" or "I activate this amulet to protect my heart as it opens to love."

2. Wearing or Carrying Your Object: Keep the talisman or amulet on your person to continuously work its magic. Wear it as a piece of jewelry, carry it in your pocket, or keep it in a safe place where you spend a lot of time.

Regularly cleanse and recharge your object, especially after a significant life event or once you feel it has done its work. This ensures it retains its power and stays aligned with your current intentions for love.

Creating and charging a talisman or amulet for love is a sacred process that combines intention, symbolism, and personal energy. Through this magical tool, you can carry your desires for love with you, drawing the energy of love closer with every step you take. Remember, the power of a talisman or amulet lies in the belief and intention you put into it.

The Use of Herbs, Oils, and Candles in Love Enchantments

In the art of love enchantments, natural elements like herbs, oils, and candles are pivotal. They serve as physical representations of our desires and intentions, each with its own energetic signature that can enhance the potency of our magical work.

Herbs have been used since ancient times for their healing properties and their ability to influence the energetic world.

1. Rose: Universally associated with love, roses can be used in any spell to draw romance and affection. Dried petals are often included in love sachets or sprinkled around a space to invite love in.

2. Lavender: Known for its calming properties, lavender promotes peace and tranquility in relationships. It can also enhance communication and mutual understanding between partners.

3. Basil: This herb is used to foster fidelity and loyalty in a relationship. It is also believed to ward off negativity and bring happiness to the home.

4. Using Herbs: Incorporate herbs into spells by creating pouches, scattering them around candles, burning them as incense, or using them to anoint candles with oil.

Oils carry the essence of the plants from which they are derived and can be used to anoint objects, people, and spaces.

1. Rose Oil: For pure love and passionate affairs, rose oil is the quintessential love attractant. Use it to anoint candles, add to baths, or wear as a personal scent.

2. Jasmine Oil: Jasmine is associated with prophetic dreams and spiritual love. It can be used to anoint the forehead before sleep to invite dreams of future loves.

3. Ylang-Ylang Oil: This oil is known for its strong sensual properties. It's excellent for deepening sexual intimacy or attracting more physical expressions of love.

4. Creating Blends: Craft your own magical oil blends by combining base oils with herbs and essential oils. Charge your blend with intention, and use it to anoint candles, talismans, or your body.

Candles provide a focal point for your intent and a means to send your wishes into the universe through flame and smoke.

1. Color Symbolism: Choose candle colors that correspond to your love intentions—pink for gentle love, red for passion, white for new beginnings, or green for nurturing love.

2. Carving and Dressing Candles: Carve symbols, names, or intentions into your candles. Dress them by rubbing them with oils, moving in one direction to draw things towards you or in the opposite direction to banish.

3. Candle Arrangements: Arrange candles in shapes that reflect your intentions, such as hearts or circles for unity. Use multiple candles to represent the various aspects of a relationship you wish to manifest or enhance.

Practical Application

When combining these elements in a love enchantment, consider the following steps:

1. Select Your Elements: Choose herbs, oils, and candle colors that align with your love intentions.

2. Prepare Your Space: Cleanse your space and create a sacred atmosphere where you can conduct your ritual without disturbances.

3. Cast Your Circle: Lay out your materials and cast a circle to create a boundary for your magical work.

4. Perform Your Ritual: Light your candles, stating your intentions. Anoint yourself with oils, focusing on opening your heart chakra. Surround your space with herbs, visualizing love blossoming in your life.

5. Seal Your Enchantment: As your candles burn down, envision your wishes rising with the smoke, being carried to the realms where magic begins to weave reality.

6. Close Your Circle: Thank any deities or energies you called upon and formally close your circle, trusting that your enchantment is now at work.

The use of herbs, oils, and candles in love enchantments is a time-honored practice, rich in symbolism and effectiveness. By carefully selecting your materials and performing your rituals with intention, you can weave powerful magic that opens the door to the love you seek. Remember, the true essence of love magic lies in the harmony between your intentions and the natural world.

Maintaining and Storing Magical Objects

Magical objects, be they talismans, amulets, enchanted jewelry, or tools like wands and athames, hold the energy of the intentions and spells they've been part of. Proper maintenance and storage of these objects are crucial to preserve their power and ensure their energies remain pure and effective for future workings.

Cleansing Your Magical Objects

Before storage, it is important to cleanse each item to rid it of any residual energies that could interfere with its potency.

1. Smudging: Pass the object through the smoke of sage, palo santo, or incense to cleanse it energetically.

2. Moonlight Bath: Place your objects under the light of the full moon to cleanse and recharge them.

3. Salt Burial: Burying objects in a bowl of salt can draw out negativity. Ensure that the material of the object is not adversely affected by salt.

4. Sound Cleansing: Use the ringing of a bell or the tones of a singing bowl to cleanse items with vibrational energy.

Once cleansed, your magical objects should be stored properly to maintain their charged energies.

1. Silk Wrapping: Wrap objects in silk, which is believed to shield against energetic intrusions.

2. Wooden Boxes: Store items in wooden boxes, which can be charged to protect the contents. Cedar, in particular, is known for its purifying properties.

3. Pouches: Use natural fabric pouches for storage, and consider adding herbs like lavender or rosemary for additional protection.

4. Separation: Store love magic items separately from objects used for protection, banishing, or other energies to prevent cross-contamination of intentions.

Establish a routine to regularly maintain your magical objects.

1. Regular Cleansing: Even while in storage, objects can accumulate energy, so regular cleansing is necessary.

2. Recharging: Periodically recharge objects by placing them in sunlight or moonlight, or by holding them during meditation and visualizing them filling with light.

3. Physical Care: Keep objects free from dust and physical debris. This is as much a practical measure as it is symbolic of keeping the objects' energies clear.

Chapter 7: Mystical Practices for Love

Meditation and Visualization Techniques for Attracting Love

Meditation and visualization are powerful techniques in the realm of love magic. They help in focusing the mind, clarifying intentions, and energetically aligning oneself with the love one seeks to attract.

Understanding Meditation and Visualization

Meditation calms the mind and centers the spirit, creating a fertile ground for the seeds of love. Visualization, a key aspect of many meditative practices, involves the creation of mental images that represent one's desires and goals. When combined, these practices can be highly effective in manifesting love.

Technique 1: Heart Chakra Meditation

The heart chakra, Anahata, is the energy center associated with love and emotional well-being.

1. Find a Quiet Space: Sit in a comfortable position in a peaceful area where you will not be disturbed.
2. Focus on the Heart Chakra: Place your hand over your heart and bring your focus to this area. Visualize a green light glowing and expanding with each breath.
3. Chant the Mantra: Silently or aloud, chant the Bija mantra associated with the heart chakra, which is "YAM."
4. Visualize Receiving Love: Imagine love flowing into your heart, healing any past wounds, and preparing you for new love.

Technique 2: Visualizing Your Ideal Partner

Visualization can help clarify what you seek in a partner and relationship.

1. Relax and Visualize: After entering a meditative state, begin to form a detailed mental image of your ideal partner. Focus on qualities, values, and the nature of the relationship rather than specific physical traits.
2. Feel the Emotions: Allow yourself to feel the emotions associated with being in this ideal relationship—joy, contentment, security, and love.
3. Release the Visualization: After spending some time in this visualization, release the image and trust that the universe will bring this love into your life in its own time.

Technique 3: Love Attraction Visualization

This technique focuses on attracting love into your life.

1. Create a Love Symbol: Start by visualizing a symbol that represents love for you. This could be a heart, a rose, or any image that resonates with love.
2. Surround Yourself with Love: Imagine this symbol surrounding you, enveloping you in its energy. Feel yourself becoming a magnet for love.
3. Daily Practice: Incorporate this visualization into your daily meditation practice to continuously attract love.

Emily, recovering from a painful breakup, used heart chakra meditation to heal her emotional wounds. Over time, she felt more open and ready for new love. She then began visualizing her ideal partner, focusing on shared values and emotional compatibility. Several months later, she met someone who embodied these qualities, and they developed a deep and loving relationship.

Astrology in Love

Astrology and divination have been used for centuries as tools to understand the self better, forecast future events, and, significantly, to navigate the complex waters of love and relationships.

Astrology offers insights into personality traits, potential compatibility, and timing for love-related decisions. It's a tool for self-discovery and understanding relational dynamics.

1. Natal Charts: Your astrological birth chart reveals your emotional needs, love language, and potential challenges in relationships. Understanding your Venus sign, for instance, can show how you give and receive love.

2. Compatibility Analysis: Synastry, or the comparison of two astrological birth charts, can highlight the strengths and challenges in a relationship, helping couples to understand and navigate their dynamics more effectively.

3. Timing for Love: Astrology can be used to identify auspicious times for love. Transits and progressions can indicate periods when the universe's energy is aligned for romance or significant relational developments.

Divination practices, such as tarot readings, runes, and pendulum dowsing, can offer guidance and clarity in matters of the heart.

1. Tarot Readings: Tarot can provide insights into current relationship dynamics, potential future love prospects, and guidance on how to navigate challenges. Love spreads can focus on specific questions or offer general insights.

2. Runes: These ancient symbols can be cast or drawn to gain insights into love-related questions, revealing underlying currents and potential outcomes.

3. Pendulum Dowsing: A pendulum can answer specific yes/no questions about love and relationships, helping to make decisions or clarify feelings.

Practical Application

1. Consult an Astrologer: For a detailed understanding of your love potential and timing, consult a professional astrologer who can analyze your birth chart and provide personalized guidance.

2. DIY Tarot Readings: Perform your own love tarot readings. Focus on clear questions and be open to the messages the cards reveal.

3. Daily Rune Casting: Cast runes each day with a question in mind about your love life. Document the symbols you draw and reflect on their meanings.

Astrology and divination are not about predicting the future with certainty but providing insights and perspectives. In the realm of love, they can be invaluable tools for understanding oneself, navigating relationships, and making informed decisions. Whether you are seeking love, in a relationship, or contemplating the next steps in your romantic journey, these ancient practices can offer clarity, comfort, and guidance.

Using Dream Work to Reveal Insights About Relationships

Dream work is a mystical and introspective practice that can offer profound insights into our subconscious desires, fears, and experiences, especially regarding love and relationships. By paying attention to our dreams and learning to interpret their symbols and narratives, we can gain a deeper understanding of our emotional landscape and relationship patterns.

Dreams often communicate through symbols, metaphors, and emotional impressions. To use dream work effectively, it is essential to become fluent in the language of your own dreams.

1. Common Symbols: While some dream symbols can be universal, such as water representing emotions or a house symbolizing the self, many symbols are unique to the individual. Over time, you can develop an understanding of what certain themes or images represent for you.

2. Emotional Resonance: Pay attention to the emotions you experience in your dreams. They can provide clues to your feelings about relationships or love situations that you might not be fully conscious of in your waking life.

Recording and Analyzing Dreams

Keeping a dream journal is a fundamental aspect of dream work. Recording your dreams as soon as you wake up helps capture details that are easily forgotten.

1. Journaling: Write down everything you can remember about your dreams, including details, emotions, colors, and even the sequence of events.

2. Analysis: Reflect on the symbols and emotions in your dream. Consider how they might relate to your current relationship experiences or desires. Look for recurring themes or patterns that could indicate deeper emotional scripts playing out in your love life.

Active Dream Work Techniques

Going beyond passive recording, there are techniques to actively engage with your dreams for deeper insights.

1. Lucid Dreaming: This is the practice of becoming conscious within your dream and being able to interact intentionally with the dream environment. Lucid

dreaming can be used to ask questions about your relationships directly within the dream.

2. Dream Incubation: Before sleeping, set an intention or ask a specific question about your love life. This can 'incubate' a dream that provides insights or answers.

3. Meditation Before Sleep: Meditate on your feelings about your relationships or love life before going to bed. This can influence the content of your dreams, making them more relevant to your current emotional concerns.

Anna was unsure about her feelings towards her partner. She began recording her dreams and noticed a recurring theme of water, which she interpreted as a symbol of her deep emotions that she hadn't fully acknowledged. This insight helped her to open up a meaningful dialogue with her partner.

Struggling with a past relationship, David practiced lucid dreaming. In his dream, he consciously confronted his ex-partner and achieved a sense of closure. This experience brought him peace in his waking life.

Dream work is a powerful tool in the quest for love and understanding in relationships. It allows access to the deeper parts of the psyche, revealing hidden feelings and thoughts. By recording, analyzing, and actively engaging with your dreams, you can uncover valuable insights that guide your decisions and actions in your waking love life. Remember, the world of dreams is a personal and subjective one; the most accurate interpretations are those that resonate deeply with your own experiences and feelings.

Part III: The Magic of Connection

Chapter 8: Strengthening Bonds

Magical Practices for Deepening Intimacy and Trust

In the journey of love, deepening intimacy and trust are essential for creating lasting and fulfilling relationships. Magical practices can be a unique and powerful way to enhance these aspects, fostering a deeper connection between partners.

Intimacy and trust are not just emotional states but energetic exchanges between individuals. By using magical practices, you can create an environment where these energies can thrive and grow.

1. Energetic Alignment: This involves aligning your energy with your partner's to foster understanding and empathy.

2. Heart Chakra Work: Focusing on the heart chakra can enhance feelings of love, compassion, and connection.

Rituals and Spells for Deepening Intimacy

1. Candle Ritual for Connection: Light a pink or green candle with your partner, symbolizing the heart chakra. As the candle burns, share your dreams, fears, and aspirations with each other. This ritual creates a safe space for emotional sharing.

2. Creating a Love Altar: Together with your partner, create an altar in your home dedicated to your relationship. Include items that represent your union, such as photographs, love letters, and symbols of shared experiences.

3. Bonding Spell: Perform a simple spell where you both write down what you appreciate about each other. Place these notes in a jar, and on each anniversary or special occasion, read them to each other, adding new notes as your relationship grows.

Visualization Techniques for Trust

1. Joint Visualization: Sit back-to-back with your partner, focusing on breathing in harmony. Visualize a circle of light encompassing you both, signifying trust and unity.

2. Trust Affirmations: Create affirmations that reinforce trust within your relationship. Recite these affirmations together regularly to create a positive and trusting mindset.

Magical Herbalism for Intimacy

1. Herbal Teas: Share a cup of herbal tea made with ingredients like rose petals (for love), jasmine (for passion), or chamomile (for harmony). This shared ritual can be a daily reminder of your commitment to nurturing your relationship.

2. Love Potpourri: Create a potpourri with herbs and flowers associated with love and trust. Keep it in your bedroom to maintain a loving and harmonious atmosphere.

Communication Spells and Rituals to Enhance Understanding

Effective communication is the cornerstone of any successful relationship. Misunderstandings, unexpressed feelings, or unsaid words can create barriers that hinder the growth of love. Magical practices can be instrumental in enhancing communication, promoting understanding, and deepening connections.

Communication in relationships goes beyond words; it encompasses the sharing of emotions, intentions, and even unspoken thoughts. By utilizing specific spells and rituals, you can open the channels of communication on a deeper, more intuitive level.

Spell 1: Throat Chakra Balancing Spell

The throat chakra governs communication and self-expression. Balancing this chakra can enhance your ability to communicate effectively.

Materials: Blue candles (representing the throat chakra); Lavender or chamomile (herbs for calming and clarity); Lapis lazuli or turquoise (stones associated with the throat chakra); A small piece of paper and a pen.

Steps:

1. Set Up: Arrange the candles, herbs, and stones in a circle.

2. Intention Writing: Write down your intention for clear and honest communication on the paper.

3. Ritual: Light the candles, hold the stones, and focus on your throat chakra. Visualize it opening and glowing with a bright blue light.

4. Affirmation: Recite an affirmation like, "My words flow freely and truthfully, promoting understanding and connection."

5. Closure: Place the paper with your intention under the candles. Let the candles burn down safely.

Spell 2: Herbal Communication Tea Ritual

Herbal teas can be used to facilitate open dialogue, especially during difficult conversations.

Materials: Herbs such as mint (for clear communication), honey (for sweetening words), and lemon balm (for calming energy); Boiling water; Two cups.

Steps:

1. Prepare the Tea: Steep the herbs in boiling water. Focus on your intention of clear and open communication as the tea brews.

2. Sharing the Tea: Share the tea with your partner before a conversation. Set the intention together to listen and speak with empathy and honesty.

Spell 3: Mercury Retrograde Communication Protection Spell

Mercury retrograde periods can often disrupt communication. This spell is designed to protect your relationship's communication during these times.

Materials: A clear quartz crystal (for clarity); A piece of paper; A small pouch.

Steps:

1. Intention Writing: Write an intention to maintain clear and loving communication even during challenging astrological times.

2. Crystal Charging: Hold the crystal, focusing on your intention. Visualize a barrier protecting your communication.

3. Pouch Preparation: Place the crystal and the paper with your intention in the pouch. Keep it close during conversations, especially in times of Mercury retrograde.

Struggling with communication in their relationship, Jake and Sarah performed the Throat Chakra Balancing Spell together. They found that this ritual helped them express their feelings more clearly and listen more effectively to each other.

Conflicts are an inevitable part of any relationship, but how they are managed can either strengthen or weaken the bond between partners. Magical practices, particularly those focusing on resolution and forgiveness, can be potent tools for mending rifts and fostering a deeper understanding.

Conflict resolution magic is about more than just ending disputes; it's about healing the underlying issues and restoring balance and harmony. It involves recognizing the root causes of conflict and addressing them on both a spiritual and emotional level.

Spell 4: Peaceful Communication Spell

A spell to promote honest and empathetic communication can be crucial in resolving misunderstandings and disagreements.

Materials: Blue candles (for calm communication); Honey (to sweeten words); Paper and pen; Lavender (for peace).

Steps:

1. Write Down Issues: Each partner writes down their perspective on the conflict.

2. Candle Ritual: Light the blue candles and place the papers next to them.

3. Recitation: Together, recite a statement of intent, such as, "With open hearts and minds, we communicate with peace and understanding."

4. Sweeten the Words: Drizzle honey over the papers as a symbol of sweetening your words and thoughts towards each other.

5. Burn the Papers: Safely burn the papers to release the grievances, allowing the lavender to smolder and spread peaceful energy.

Spell 5: Forgiveness Magic Ritual

Forgiveness is a powerful act that can release both parties from the chains of resentment and hurt.

Materials: White candles (for purity and new beginnings); Rose quartz (for heart healing); A bowl of water (for emotional cleansing); Sage (for purification).

Steps:

1. Cleanse the Space: Begin by smudging the area with sage.

2. Candle Lighting: Light the white candles, focusing on the intention to forgive and be forgiven.

3. Rose Quartz Holding: Each partner holds a piece of rose quartz, channeling thoughts of forgiveness and understanding.

4. Water Ritual: Take turns washing each other's hands in the bowl of water, symbolizing the washing away of hurt and resentment.

5. Affirmation of Forgiveness: Together, recite an affirmation of forgiveness, such as, "We choose to forgive and move forward with love and understanding."

A Magical Approach to Attracting a Man's Attention in Communication

You can also incorporate magic into everyday communication and resort to proven communication methods. This, combined with rituals, will enhance the quality of your relationships.

Step 1: Initial Interaction

Energetic Mirroring: Before the meeting, tune into positive energy. Take a few deep breaths, envisioning your aura being filled with light. Observe the man's gestures and manner of speaking, and discreetly mirror them, creating a subconscious sense of similarity.

Magic of Open Questions: Use questions to deepen the conversation: "What inspires you about this hobby?" or "What impressions did you have from your last trip?"

Step 2: Creating an Emotional Connection

Maintaining Positive Energy: Keep the focus on positive topics. Avoid negative or controversial topics that could create heavy energy. Laugh and smile, spreading light energy.

Magic of Listening and Reflecting: Listen attentively, maintaining eye contact and nodding in understanding. Reflect and affirm his thoughts, using phrases like "I completely understand why you think that."

Step 3: Deep Energetic Communication

Using Magical Symbols and Signs: Ask questions that require open responses, and listen attentively. Use symbolic gestures, such as a nod or a smile, to maintain the connection.

Emotional Disclosure: Share a story from your life that shows your vulnerability or passion. This helps to create emotional closeness.

Step 4: Using Body Language

Magic of Eye Contact: Establish and maintain moderate eye contact during conversation, showing your interest and attention. Avoid prolonged intense stares to prevent discomfort.

Light Physical Contact: Use casual, unobtrusive touch, like touching his hand during laughter, to strengthen the connection.

Step 5: Enhancing Interest

Energy of Spontaneity: Be open to unexpected suggestions and adventures, showing your flexibility and love of life. Suggest interesting and unusual ways to spend time together.

Demonstrating Unique Energetic Qualities: Highlight your unique traits that set you apart, whether it be hobbies, talents, or beliefs.

Step 6: Creating Psycho-Energetic Closeness

Joint Energetic Decision-Making: Involve him in the discussion of plans and events, emphasizing the importance of his opinion and choice.

Energetic Support and Care: Show care and support for his energetic needs, interests, and problems.

Step 7: Maintaining and Deepening the Connection

Regular Energetic Communication: Maintain a constant flow of communication, showing interest in his life and experiences.

Spending Time Together: Spend time together in various settings to strengthen and deepen your bond. Try to create shared memories by being in places or doing things that evoke strong emotions.

Step 8: Establishing a Long-Term Connection

Honest Expression of Energetic Feelings: Frankly express your feelings and intentions, discussing your emotions and future prospects.

Joint Energetic Future Planning: Discuss your joint plans and dreams, planning the future together.

Chapter 9: Keeping the Flame Alive

Magic for Rekindling Passion and Interest

In long-term relationships, it's natural for the initial intensity of passion and interest to ebb and flow. However, when these vital elements wane significantly, it can affect the overall health and happiness of the partnership. Fortunately, magical practices can be employed to reignite these flames and bring a renewed sense of excitement and connection.

Passion magic is about reigniting the spark of desire and intrigue. It involves tapping into the primal energies of attraction and excitement, helping couples to rediscover the joy and exhilaration that initially brought them together.

Passion Candle Spell

This spell uses the transformative power of fire to reignite passion.

Materials: Red candles (symbolizing passion and desire); Cinnamon oil (for heat and quick action); Paper and pen.

Steps:

1. Intention Setting: Write down your desires for your relationship on the paper. Be specific about the kind of passion and interests you want to reawaken.

2. Candle Preparation: Anoint the candles with cinnamon oil, moving from the base to the wick, to draw energy in.

3. Ritual: Light the candles and focus on the flames. Visualize the heat and energy reigniting the passion in your relationship.

4. Affirmation: Recite an affirmation like, "Our relationship is ablaze with passion and intrigue."

Sensual Bath Ritual

Water is a powerful element for cleansing and rejuvenation, making it ideal for renewing passion.

Materials: Warm bath water; Rose petals (for love and romance); Jasmine or ylang-ylang oil (for sensuality); Pink or red candles.

Steps:

1. Bath Preparation: Fill the bath with warm water and add the rose petals and a few drops of jasmine or ylang-ylang oil.

2. Ambiance: Light the candles around the bath to create a sensual and relaxing atmosphere.

3. Bath Ritual: Share the bath with your partner, focusing on relaxing and reconnecting. Use this time to communicate your desires and appreciation for each other.

Passionate Dance Ritual

Dance is a primal and expressive way to reconnect physically and emotionally.

Materials: A playlist of music that you both find energizing or romantic; An open space free from interruption.

Steps:

1. Setting the Scene: Create a comfortable and inviting space to dance. This could be in your living room or even outdoors under the stars.

2. Dancing Together: Start the music and dance together. Let the rhythm guide you, focusing on the movement and physical connection with your partner.

Rekindling passion and interest in a relationship through magic is about creating intentional spaces and actions that remind you of the love and desire you have for each other. Whether it's through a candle spell, a shared bath, or a dance, the key is to focus on the connection and the unique bond you share. These magical practices are not just about reigniting physical passion; they're also about nurturing the emotional and spiritual aspects of your relationship, ensuring a well-rounded and fulfilling partnership.

Celebratory Rituals for Anniversaries and Special Occasions

Anniversaries and special occasions are milestones that mark the journey of love and commitment. Celebrating these moments with magical rituals can infuse your relationship with renewed energy, gratitude, and joy. Celebratory rituals in love magic are not just about marking a date on the calendar. They are a conscious acknowledgment of the journey two people have shared, honoring both the joys and challenges that have strengthened their bond.

Love Renewal Ritual

This ritual is about reaffirming your commitment and love for each other, suitable for anniversaries or any significant moment in your relationship.

Materials: Two white candles (symbolizing purity and new beginnings); A piece of paper and pen for each person; A bowl of water with rose petals; A small gift or token of love.

Steps:

1. Preparation: Write down what you cherish about your partner and your hopes for the future together.

2. Ritual: Light the candles and face each other. Take turns reading what you've written, acknowledging the past and future.

3. Exchange Tokens: Exchange your gifts or tokens as a physical representation of your renewed commitment.

4. Closing: Place the papers in the bowl of water, letting the words and rose petals blend together, symbolizing the blending of your lives.

Memory Creation Ritual

This ritual focuses on creating new, positive memories to add to your shared history.

Materials: A special item that holds significance to both of you (e.g., a photo from a memorable day); A box or container; Various small items that represent your goals and dreams as a couple.

Steps:

1. Collection: Together, gather items that represent your shared experiences and aspirations.

2. Memory Box: Place these items in your chosen box or container, focusing on the memories they represent and the future they symbolize.

3. Sealing the Box: Close the box, and decide on a future date when you will open it again, perhaps on your next anniversary.

Gratitude and Vision Ritual

Gratitude is a powerful emotion that can strengthen the bond between partners. This ritual combines gratitude with visioning for the future.

Materials: Comfortable seating in a quiet space; Soft music and candles; A journal.

Steps:

1. Gratitude Sharing: Sit together and share things you are grateful for in your relationship. Be specific and genuine.

2. Visioning: Discuss your visions for the future – where you see yourselves, what you wish to achieve, and how you want to grow together.

3. Journaling: Write these visions in your journal, creating a physical record of your shared dreams.

Celebratory rituals offer a magical way to honor the path you've walked as a couple and to energize your journey ahead. They are a testament to the enduring nature of love and a reminder of the shared commitment that sustains a relationship. Whether it's a grand gesture or a simple, intimate moment, these rituals deepen the connection and add a layer of sacredness to your celebration.

Part IV: Overcoming Love's Challenges

Chapter 10: Navigating Relationship Challenges

When to Use Magic and When to Seek Mundane Solutions

Navigating the balance between magical interventions and practical, "mundane" solutions in love and relationships is crucial. While magic can offer powerful tools for enhancing and healing relationships, it's important to recognize its limits and understand when more conventional approaches are needed. Magic, in the context of love and relationships, is about setting intentions, aligning energies, and creating an environment conducive to romance and connection. It can help to:

1. Shift Perspectives: Magic can provide a fresh viewpoint, allowing you to see relationship issues in a new light.

2. Enhance Energy: Rituals and spells can bolster personal energy or the energy within a relationship.

3. Open Pathways: Magical practices can open pathways for communication, understanding, and love.

However, it's essential to recognize that magic is a tool, not a panacea. It works best when coupled with real-world actions and solutions.

Knowing When to Use Magic

1. Deepening Connections: Use magical practices when looking to enhance or deepen an already healthy relationship.

2. Personal Growth and Reflection: Magic is useful for personal growth, self-discovery, and understanding your role in a relationship.

3. Overcoming Minor Obstacles: For small hurdles in a relationship, magic can be a supportive tool.

Identifying When Mundane Solutions Are Needed

1. Communication Issues: While magic can help open lines of communication, actual conversation and active listening are necessary for resolving issues.

2. Fundamental Differences: Major issues like vastly different life goals, values, or views on significant matters often require practical discussions or counseling.

3. Emotional and Physical Well-Being: Issues concerning mental health, emotional stability, or physical well-being should be addressed with professional help.

Balancing Magic with Mundane

1. Complementary Approaches: Use magic to set the stage for love and growth, but pair it with practical actions. For instance, a spell for open communication pairs well with setting aside time each day to talk without distractions.

2. Professional Guidance: Sometimes, the best approach is a combination of magic and professional advice, such as counseling or relationship coaching.

Magic can be a beautiful and effective way to enhance your love life, but it's important to recognize its scope and limitations. In matters of the heart, a balanced approach that combines magical practices with practical, real-world actions often yields the best results. Remember, the key to a successful relationship lies in a blend of the mystical and the mundane, where magic sets the tone and everyday actions build the story.

Protection Spells for Safeguarding Love

In the journey of love and relationships, safeguarding the bond you share with your partner is just as important as nurturing it. Protection spells in love magic are designed to shield your relationship from external negativity, misunderstandings, and internal conflicts that could harm your bond. Protection spells for love are not about creating an unrealistic barrier against all challenges. Instead, they are about fortifying the relationship against unnecessary negative influences and fostering resilience.

Circle of Protection Spell

This spell creates a symbolic circle of protection around your relationship.

Materials: White candles (for purity and protection); Salt (for grounding and protection); A piece of paper and pen; Lavender or rosemary (for peace and clarity).

Steps:

1. Create Your Circle: Arrange the white candles and sprinkle salt in a circle.

2. State Your Intentions: Write down your intention to protect your relationship. Place this paper in the center of the circle.

3. Light the Candles: As you light each candle, visualize a protective light surrounding your relationship.

4. Ritual Affirmation: Recite an affirmation like, "Our relationship is safeguarded against all harm and flourishes in love and trust."

Amulet of Love Protection

Creating an amulet can provide ongoing protection for your relationship.

Materials: A small pouch; Protective stones like black tourmaline or obsidian (for absorbing negativity); Rose petals (for love); A personal item from each partner (to represent the bond).

Steps:

1. Assemble the Amulet: Place the stones, rose petals, and personal items in the pouch.

2. Charge the Amulet: Hold the amulet in your hands, visualizing a protective energy enveloping your relationship.

3. Finalize: Keep the amulet in a shared space, such as your bedroom, to maintain the protective energy.

Shielding Visualization Ritual

Visualization is a powerful tool in creating an energetic shield around your relationship.

Materials: Quiet space; Comfortable seating; Focus and intention.

Steps:

1. Relax and Visualize: Sit comfortably and close your eyes. Breathe deeply and center yourself.

2. Energetic Shielding: Imagine an orb of protective light surrounding you and your partner, repelling negativity and fostering love and understanding.

3. Seal the Visualization: End the visualization with a statement of gratitude for the protection of your relationship.

Protection spells and rituals in love magic are about creating a sacred space where your relationship can thrive safely. They are a way of energetically asserting that your bond is valued and guarded. By regularly performing these protective practices, you and your partner can reinforce your commitment to each other and foster a relationship resilient in the face of both internal and external pressures. Remember, the strength of these spells lies in the intention and the belief behind them – a testament to the power of your love and commitment to protect it.

Letting Go and Moving On: Dealing with Unrequited Love Through Magic

Unrequited love is a deeply challenging experience, often laden with intense emotions and a profound sense of loss. However, it also offers an opportunity for significant personal growth and transformation. Magic can be a compassionate and empowering tool to aid in the process of letting go and moving on from unrequited love. The magic of releasing unrequited love is about acknowledging and honoring your feelings while also gently severing the emotional cords that bind you to a situation that is not serving your highest good.

Cord-Cutting Ritual

This ritual symbolizes and facilitates the energetic cutting of ties with the object of your unrequited love.

Materials: Black or white candle (for purification and new beginnings); A piece of string or yarn (representing the emotional ties); Scissors or a ritual knife (for cutting the string); A small bowl of water (for emotional cleansing).

Steps:

1. Preparation: Light the candle and place the string in front of you, visualizing it as the connection you wish to sever.

2. Ritual Act: Cut the string with scissors or a ritual knife while affirming your intention to release the attachment and move forward. For example, say, "I release this bond and open my heart to new possibilities."

3. Cleansing: Pass the cut string through the flame (carefully) and then place it in the water, symbolizing purification and emotional healing.

4. Closing: Allow the candle to burn down safely, signifying the end of the attachment.

Releasing Spell with Fire

Fire is a powerful element for transformation and can be used to burn away lingering feelings of unrequited love.

Materials: Fire-safe bowl or cauldron; Paper and pen; Dried herbs like sage or rosemary (for cleansing and healing).

Steps:

1. Writing Down Feelings: Write down your feelings about the unrequited love on the paper. Be honest and thorough.

2. Burning Ceremony: Place the paper in the bowl and set it alight, allowing the flames to consume your written words. As it burns, imagine your feelings being transformed by the fire.

3. Herbal Cleanse: Add the dried herbs to the fire, letting their smoke signify the clearing of old energies and the welcoming of new beginnings.

Self-Love and Healing Ritual

Focusing on self-love is crucial in overcoming unrequited love. This ritual helps redirect love and energy back to yourself.

Materials: Pink candle (for self-love); Rose quartz (for heart healing); Lavender oil (for calming and peace); A mirror.

Steps:

1. Candle Lighting: Light the pink candle and anoint yourself with lavender oil.

2. Mirror Work: Sit in front of the mirror, holding the rose quartz. Look into your eyes and affirm your worthiness of love. For example, say, "I am worthy of love and I give love to myself."

3. Meditation: Close your eyes and meditate on the qualities you love about yourself, allowing the energy of the rose quartz to amplify these feelings.

Dealing with unrequited love is a deeply personal and often painful process, but it also provides a powerful opportunity for growth and self-discovery. Utilizing magical practices to let go and move on can be a gentle yet effective way to navigate this challenging experience. Rituals for closure from past relationships are an essential step in the healing process, allowing you to sever old ties, heal emotional wounds, and prepare for future love. These practices provide a symbolic, yet powerful, way to acknowledge the end of one chapter and the beginning of another. They offer not just an emotional release but also a spiritual cleansing, paving the way for new, healthy, and fulfilling relationships. Remember, the journey of healing and moving forward is deeply personal, it's about honoring your feelings, learning from your experiences, and embracing the growth that comes from change.

Part V: Ethical Considerations and Advanced Practices

Chapter 11: The Ethics of Love Magic

Discussion on the Moral Implications of Love Spells

When delving into the realm of love magic, it is crucial to consider the ethical and moral implications of such practices. Love spells, while often sought for their perceived ability to influence romantic outcomes, tread a delicate line between personal desire and ethical conduct. The ethics of love magic hinge on the principles of consent and free will. It's essential to recognize that any spell or magical practice that aims to override another person's free will or manipulate their emotions is ethically questionable.

Consent and Free Will

In the context of love spells, consent refers to the acknowledgment and respect of the other person's autonomy and decision-making capacity. Love spells that aim to coerce, manipulate, or change the feelings of another without their awareness or consent are problematic from an ethical standpoint.

The Law of Threefold Return

Many magical traditions adhere to the belief in the Law of Threefold Return, which suggests that whatever energy a person puts out into the world, whether positive or negative, will be returned to them threefold. This is particularly important to consider when performing any spell, especially those concerning love.

Self-Reflection and Intention

Before casting a love spell, it is crucial to engage in self-reflection. Understanding your intentions and the potential impact of your actions is vital. Spells that focus on self-improvement, confidence, and opening oneself to the possibility of love are generally more ethically sound than those targeting specific individuals.

Love Spells and Karma

Another consideration is the concept of karma, or the spiritual principle of cause and effect. Interfering with someone else's free will might have unforeseen karmic repercussions, affecting not just the target of the spell but also the one who casts it.

Case of Unrequited Love: Sarah considered using a love spell on her crush but realized it would be unethical to try to manipulate his feelings. Instead, she chose a spell to enhance her self-confidence and openness to love, which ultimately led her to a fulfilling relationship with someone else.

Enhancing Existing Love: Tom and Linda, a couple experiencing a rough patch, jointly decided to use a spell to enhance communication and understanding in their relationship. This mutual agreement and shared intention aligned with ethical practices in love magic.

The practice of love spells requires careful ethical consideration. The key is to focus on spells and rituals that enhance personal attributes, create opportunities for love, and respect the autonomy and free will of others. Love magic, when practiced with pure intentions and ethical considerations, can be a beautiful and enriching experience. However, it's important to remember that the most powerful magic often lies not in changing others but in transforming ourselves and how we interact with the world.

Respecting Free Will and Consent in Magical Practices

In the pursuit of love and companionship, it is paramount to approach magical practices with an ethos that respects the principles of free will and consent. The essence of ethical love magic lies in its alignment with the principles of harmlessness and respect for individual sovereignty. It is essential to understand that true love cannot be forced, and any attempt to control or manipulate another's emotions or free will contradicts the foundational principles of love and respect.

Free will is the fundamental right of every individual to make their own choices and decisions. In love magic, this means any spell or ritual should not aim to coerce, manipulate, or override the free will of another person. The focus should always be on self-improvement and creating an environment conducive to love, rather than attempting to direct the will of another.

Consent in magical practices refers to the conscious agreement of all parties involved. In the context of love spells, this means that performing spells directly affecting another person without their knowledge or consent is ethically questionable. It is always preferable to engage in spells and rituals that focus on self-development and attraction, rather than those targeting specific individuals.

Focusing on spells and rituals that enhance one's own attractiveness, confidence, and open-heartedness is a way to respect free will. For example, spells for self-love, confidence, or attractiveness to draw the right person into your life align with ethical practices.

The intention behind a spell or ritual is crucial. Setting intentions that are focused on personal growth and the natural attraction of love, rather than seeking to bend another's will to one's desires, is key to ethical magical practice.

Emily, after several unsuccessful relationships, turned to love magic. She chose to perform a self-love ritual, enhancing her self-esteem and personal joy. This shift in focus brought a new sense of fulfillment and eventually led her to a loving relationship that formed naturally.

Alex and Jordan, a couple seeking to deepen their connection, jointly decided to engage in a ritual to enhance communication and understanding in their relationship. Their mutual consent and shared intention made the ritual a beautiful and ethical expression of their commitment.

Navigating love magic with a respect for free will and consent is not only an ethical imperative but also a path to more genuine and fulfilling romantic experiences. By focusing on personal growth and natural attraction rather than coercion or manipulation, practitioners can engage in a form of love magic that honors the autonomy of all individuals involved. This approach ensures that the love attracted is based on mutual respect, genuine connection, and free choice, laying the foundation for a relationship built on trust and mutual understanding.

Understanding the Moral Implications of Influencing Will

In the realm of love and magic, the question of influencing another person's will is a complex and morally charged issue. This chapter delves into the ethical considerations of using magical practices to influence the will, particularly in the context of romantic relationships. It aims to provide a nuanced understanding of the moral implications involved and guides practitioners in making ethically sound choices in their magical endeavors.

At the heart of ethical magical practice is the principle of not infringing upon another person's free will. This principle is crucial when it comes to love magic, where the line between influence and manipulation can often become blurred.

Free will is a fundamental human right, entailing the freedom to make choices without coercion or undue influence. In love magic, respecting free will means avoiding any spell or ritual designed to manipulate or control another person's feelings or decisions.

Many magical traditions abide by some version of the Law of Return, which posits that whatever energy or intention you put out into the world will return to you. This is especially important to consider in the context of love spells, as manipulating someone's will could have unintended karmic consequences.

Consent is a key factor in ethical magical practices. Spells that target specific individuals to elicit romantic feelings or attraction without their knowledge or consent are considered ethically problematic. The focus should instead be on spells that attract love in a more general sense or work on enhancing one's own qualities.

The intention behind a spell is crucial. Practitioners must consider whether their intentions are for the highest good of all involved. Responsible magic involves self-reflection and an honest assessment of one's motivations.

Case of Unintended Consequences: A practitioner cast a spell to make a specific person fall in love with them. While the spell initially seemed successful, it eventually led to negative consequences for both parties, as the relationship was founded on artificially influenced feelings, not genuine mutual affection.

Ethical Alternative: Another individual chose to perform a spell focused on opening their heart to love and enhancing their own attractiveness, both physically and emotionally. This approach led to a healthy and consensual relationship founded on genuine mutual attraction and respect.

Navigating Ethical Dilemmas

In cases where the ethical path is unclear, practitioners should:

Consult their intuition and moral compass: Take time to reflect deeply on the potential impact of their actions.

Seek guidance: Consult with more experienced practitioners or turn to respected texts and teachings for insight.

The Karmic Considerations of Love Spells

In the practice of love magic, it's vital to consider the karmic implications of spells and enchantments. Karma, a concept found in various spiritual traditions, refers to the cycle of cause and effect, where the actions of an individual influence their future.

The principle of karma is not just about retribution or punishment; it's about the balance and harmony of the universe. Every action, intention, and energy put forth in a spell or ritual can return to the practitioner in some form.

In many magical traditions, especially within Wicca and Neopaganism, there is a belief in the Law of Threefold Return. This law suggests that whatever energy a practitioner puts out into the world, whether good or bad, will return to them three times over. This is particularly pertinent in love spells, where the intentions and energies are complex and potent.

Love spells can tread a fine line between influence and manipulation. Ethical considerations in love magic involve:

Respecting Free Will: Avoiding spells that attempt to coerce or dominate another person's will or emotions.

Positive Intentions: Focusing on spells that invite love in a general sense, or work on self-improvement and readiness for love, rather than targeting a specific individual.

Karma-friendly love spells are those that:

- Enhance Personal Attractiveness: Spells that work on making the practitioner more open, loving, and ready for a healthy relationship.

- Attract Love Naturally: Spells that set the intention to attract love into one's life without specifying or targeting a particular person.

- Heal from Past Relationships: Spells that assist in letting go of past baggage, healing emotional wounds, and preparing for new love.

Mia's Self-Love Spell: After several unsuccessful relationships, Mia performed a self-love spell. This practice helped her attract a partner who appreciated her for who she truly was, demonstrating the positive return of her good intentions.

Liam's Attraction Spell: Liam cast a spell to enhance his own romantic allure without targeting anyone specific. He met his future partner naturally, with their relationship evolving organically, reflecting the ethical nature of his spell.

Navigating Karmic Implications

- Reflection Before Casting: Before performing a love spell, practitioners should reflect on their intentions and potential karmic consequences.

- Seeking Guidance: Consulting with more experienced practitioners or spiritual guides can provide clarity on the karmic implications of certain spells.

Karmic considerations play a crucial role in the practice of love spells. By focusing on ethical practices that respect free will and foster positive intentions, practitioners can work in harmony with the laws of karma. This approach not only ensures ethical compliance but also aligns with the higher purpose of love magic: to bring love, joy, and harmony into one's life. Remember, in love magic, as in all magical practices, the energies you send out into the universe will shape your own experiences in return.

Chapter 12: Advanced Magical Work

Working with Deities and Spirits in Love Magic

Incorporating deities and spirits into love magic can add a profound dimension to your practice. Many cultures and traditions recognize divine or spiritual entities that govern aspects of love, passion, and relationships. Deities and spirits in love magic are often invoked for their guidance, blessings, or intervention in matters of the heart. Each deity or spirit may have specific associations, attributes, and myths that make them particularly potent for different aspects of love and relationships.

Identifying the Right Deities or Spirits

- Research and select deities or spirits aligned with your intentions in love. For example, Venus or Aphrodite for romantic love, Freya for passion and fertility, or Parvati for marital harmony.

- Understand their myths, symbols, and preferred offerings to ensure your approach aligns with their traditional worship.

Creating an Altar

- Dedicate a space in your home for an altar to the chosen deity or spirit. Decorate it with symbols, images, or items that represent the entity.

- Regularly offer items that are believed to be favored by the deity or spirit, such as flowers, incense, or food.

Rituals and Offerings

- Perform rituals that honor the chosen deity or spirit, incorporating chanting, meditation, or the recitation of specific prayers or invocations.

- Offerings are a way to show respect and gratitude. These can include candles, food, libations, or other items considered sacred to the deity or spirit.

Meditation and Communication

- Spend time in meditation at your altar, seeking guidance or assistance in your love life.

- Be open to receiving messages, which may come in various forms such as dreams, signs, or intuitive feelings.

Ava, seeking to attract romantic love, set up an altar dedicated to Venus. She offered roses and perfumes and recited ancient hymns in honor of the goddess. Over time, she felt a greater sense of self-love and soon entered into a loving relationship.

Michael performed a ritual invoking Eros to rekindle passion in his marriage. He used traditional Greek offerings and prayers, which he felt helped to significantly deepen the bond between him and his partner.

Ethical Considerations

- Always approach deities and spirits with respect and reverence. Remember that you are requesting their assistance, not demanding it.

- Be mindful of the cultural context of the deities and spirits you are working with. Ensure that your practices honor and respect their origins and traditions.

Working with deities and spirits in love magic can be a powerful and enriching practice. It requires a combination of respect, knowledge, and openness to the spiritual dimensions of love. By building a relationship with these entities, you can gain valuable insights and assistance in your romantic endeavors. However, always remember that the core of this work is cooperation and reverence, never coercion or control.

Creating Long-Term Talismans for Love and Relationship Stability

In the pursuit of lasting love and relationship harmony, talismans can serve as powerful tools. These enchanted objects are charged with specific intentions and energies, designed to support and strengthen romantic bonds over time. Talismans in love magic are more than mere symbols; they are energetic reservoirs that embody your intentions for love and relationship stability. When created and used properly, they can act as anchors, continually drawing in and radiating the energies they are imbued with.

1. Selecting Your Talisman

- Choose an object that resonates with love and harmony. This could be a piece of jewelry, a natural stone like rose quartz or jade, a written symbol, or any item that holds personal significance.

- The chosen talisman should feel intuitively right for your purpose.

2. Cleansing and Preparing the Talisman

- Before charging your talisman, it must be cleansed of any previous energies. This can be done through smudging with sage, burying in salt, bathing in moonlight, or other cleansing rituals.

- After cleansing, hold the talisman in your hands and meditate on your intention for it. Visualize it becoming a vessel for your desired energies.

3. Charging the Talisman

- Charging can be done in various ways, including placing the talisman under a full moon, anointing it with oils associated with love (such as rose or ylang-ylang), or passing it through the smoke of incense.

- While charging, clearly state your intentions, whether it's attracting love, enhancing communication in your relationship, or fostering harmony and understanding.

4. Activation Ritual

- Perform a simple activation ritual to awaken the energies within the talisman. This can involve reciting a specific affirmation or prayer, visualizing a bright light enveloping the talisman, or other personal rituals that resonate with your intention.

- Example Affirmation: "I activate this talisman as a beacon and guardian of love and harmony in my life."

5. Using and Maintaining the Talisman

- Keep the talisman close to you, especially in situations where you wish to draw upon its energies. It can be worn, carried in a pocket, or kept in a special place in your home.

- Regularly cleanse and recharge the talisman to maintain its potency. This is especially important during significant relationship milestones or challenges.

Real-Life Applications

- Emma's Rose Quartz Pendant: Emma chose a rose quartz pendant as a talisman to attract a loving relationship. She cleansed and charged it under a full moon with the intention of drawing love into her life. Within months, she found a partner who resonated with the qualities she had visualized.

- Liam and Grace's Harmony Stone**: For their anniversary, Liam and Grace selected a jade stone as their talisman for relationship harmony. They charged it together, focusing on their shared goals and love. They keep it in their bedroom to maintain a peaceful and loving atmosphere.

Creating and utilizing long-term talismans in love magic can be a deeply personal and powerful practice. These talismans serve as continual reminders and vessels of your intentions for love and relationship stability. By treating them with respect and regularly reaffirming their purpose, they can become enduring allies in your journey of love and companionship. Remember, the true power of a talisman lies in the energy and intent invested in it.

Afterword and Conclusion

As we close the pages of "Magic & Love. Magical Match," it is my hope that this journey through the realms of practical magic, love spells, enchantments, and mystical practices has been enlightening and empowering. The path of magical love is rich and varied, encompassing not only the spells and rituals that we have explored but also the deeper understanding of ourselves and our relationships.

Throughout this book, we have navigated the delicate balance between magical influence and ethical practice, emphasizing the importance of consent, free will, and personal responsibility. We have delved into the complexities of working with deities and spirits, the significance of karmic considerations, and the power of intention in all magical workings.

One of the most significant lessons we hope you take away from this book is the integration of magical practices into your daily life. Magic is not just for special occasions or times of need; it is a way of living, a lens through which we can view the world and our relationships. By infusing your daily life with intention and a touch of magic, you can transform the mundane into something truly extraordinary.

Another critical aspect of your magical journey is the commitment to continual growth and learning. The world of magic is vast and ever-evolving, and so too should be your practice. Stay curious, open-minded, and willing to explore new facets of magical practice. Remember, your growth in magic parallels your growth in love and life.

At the heart of all these practices, spells, and rituals is love. Love is the most powerful magic of all, capable of transforming lives, healing wounds, and bringing unparalleled joy. Whether you are seeking new love, nurturing an existing relationship, or learning to love yourself more deeply, know that the magic you seek is within you. It is in your intentions, your actions, your beliefs, and your capacity to give and receive love.

I extend my deepest gratitude to you, the reader, for embarking on this journey with me. May the spells, rituals, and wisdom contained within these pages enrich your life and relationships. May your path in love and magic be blessed with joy, growth, and deep fulfillment.

As we conclude "Magic & Love. Magical Match," remember that this is not an end but a beginning. Your magical journey in love continues beyond these pages, into the vast and wondrous expanse of your life. May you walk this path with an open heart, a clear mind, and the courage to embrace all the magic that life and love have to offer.

With love and magical blessings,
Annabel Arno

Appendices

A Glossary of Magical Terms

As you navigate through the enchanting world of "Magic & Love. Magical Match," you'll encounter various magical terms that are essential to understanding and practicing the art of love magic. This glossary is designed to provide clarity and deepen your knowledge of these key terms.

1. Affirmation: A positive statement or declaration, often used in spells and rituals, to manifest a desired outcome.

2. Altar: A sacred space set aside for performing magical rituals and spells, often decorated with items significant to the practitioner's intentions.

3. Amulet: An object believed to have the power to protect its holder from harm or negative energy.

4. Athame: A ceremonial blade used in magical practices, symbolizing the element of air and the power of discernment.

5. Aura: The energy field that surrounds every being, often seen as an emanation of spiritual energy.

6. Casting a Circle: A ritual act of creating a protective and sacred space for conducting magical work.

7. Chakra: Points within the body in Eastern spiritual traditions, each corresponding to different aspects of physical and spiritual well-being.

8. Enchantment: A spell or magical act designed to imbue an object or person with specific magical properties or influences.

9. Energetic Cord: An invisible link formed between individuals, through which emotional and spiritual energy can be exchanged or influenced.

10. Invocation: The act of calling upon a deity, spirit, or other supernatural entity during a ritual or spell.

11. Karma: A spiritual principle of cause and effect, where intentions and actions influence the future.

12. Law of Threefold Return: A belief, particularly in Wicca, that whatever energy a person puts out into the world, whether positive or negative, will return to them threefold.

13. Pendulum: A tool used for divination, consisting of a weighted object suspended on a chain or cord.

14. Ritual: A series of actions performed in a ceremonial manner, often with specific symbolic significance.

15. Smudging: The act of burning sacred herbs, such as sage, to cleanse a space or person of negative energy.

16. Spell: A magical formula or set of actions intended to bring about a specific outcome.

17. Talisman: An object believed to bring good luck or have other positive effects, often inscribed with symbols or charged with specific energy.

18. Visualization: The practice of forming mental images, used in magic to focus and direct energy towards a desired outcome.

19. Wicca: A modern Pagan religion that incorporates certain magical practices and the worship of a Goddess and God.

20. Yin and Yang: A concept in Chinese philosophy, representing the duality and interdependence of opposite forces in the universe.

This glossary provides a foundation for understanding the magical terms. As you delve deeper into the world of love magic, these terms will become familiar tools in your journey of enchantment and romantic discovery.

Step-by-Step Guides for Rituals and Spells

"Magic & Love. Magical Match" is designed to be a practical guide for those seeking to enhance their romantic lives through the art of magic. This section provides detailed, step-by-step instructions for various rituals and spells, helping you harness the power of love magic in your life.

1. Ritual for Attracting Love

Materials Needed: Pink candle; Rose quartz; Lavender oil; A piece of paper and pen.

Steps:

1. Set your space: Create a calm, quiet area for your ritual. Cleanse the space using sage or incense.

2. Candle preparation: Anoint the pink candle with lavender oil, focusing on your intention to attract love.

3. Activation: Light the candle and hold the rose quartz in your hand.

4. Write your intention: On the piece of paper, write down the qualities you seek in a partner or relationship.

5. Visualization: Close your eyes and visualize these qualities manifesting in your life. Feel the emotions associated with this love.

6. Affirmation: Recite an affirmation such as, "I am open and ready to receive love."

7. Close the ritual: Extinguish the candle safely. Keep the rose quartz and the written intention in a special place.

2. Spell for Deepening Existing Love

Materials Needed: Two red candles; Jasmine incense; A photo of you and your partner.

Steps:

1. Prepare your altar: Place the photo at the center of your altar, flanked by the two red candles.
2. Light the candles and incense: As you do so, focus on the flame and the scent, letting them symbolize the warmth and depth of your relationship.
3. Join energies: If possible, perform this ritual with your partner. Hold hands and gaze at the photo, reminiscing about happy memories together.
4. Share affirmations: Take turns expressing what you cherish about each other and your relationship.
5. Seal the spell: Blow out the candles together, visualizing your love growing stronger.
6. Closure: Place the photo in a place where you both can see it daily as a reminder of your bond.

3. Cord-Cutting Ritual for Moving On

Materials Needed: Black candle; A piece of cord or string; Scissors; Salt.

Steps:

1. Space preparation: Create a quiet space where you won't be disturbed. Sprinkle salt in a circle around you for protection.
2. Candle lighting: Light the black candle, focusing on your intention to release past attachments.
3. Cord representation: Hold the cord, visualizing it as the emotional tie to your past relationship.
4. Cutting the cord: With the scissors, decisively cut the cord while affirming, "I release the past and open myself to new beginnings."
5. Finalize the ritual: Let the candle burn out safely. Dispose of the cord pieces outside of your home, symbolizing the release of the attachment.

These step-by-step guides provide a framework for you to engage with love magic effectively. As you perform these rituals and spells, remember that the most potent ingredient is your intention and emotional investment. With practice and sincerity, these magical practices can become powerful tools in your journey of love and romance.

Made in the USA
Las Vegas, NV
27 March 2025